How Can
I Live
Effectively?

How Can
I Live
Effectively?

CHARLES E. BLAIR

Foreword by J. Sidlow Baxter

ZONDERVAN Publishing House

GRAND RAPIDS, MICHIGAN

FOREWORD

It is an honor to write this brief foreword for my friend, Dr. Charles E. Blair of Calvary Temple, Denver, Colorado. His outstanding ministry in and from that great city is now widely known, and has promise of yet larger expansion. Quite apart from its intrinsic value, this book has three features which make it unique: (1) It coincides with Dr. Blair's twentieth anniversary in the pastorate of Calvary Temple, which, under his gifted leadership, has developed from a mere handful of members into one of the largest evangelical churches in the U.S.A. (2) This is the first book Dr. Blair has published; and, if his ministry by pen is to develop as his ministry in the pulpit, then this book has prophetic significance. (3) Unlike most books, this one does not originate solely in the author's mind, but in questions asked of him by over five thousand *others* in response to a public questionnaire issued to find out which are the questions uppermost in people's minds concerning things Christian and spiritual.

This book gives the author's answers to the *top* questions! Perhaps the highest compliment I can pay is to say that the answers are characteristic of the man. There is nothing abstruse or misty. The answers are Scriptural, direct, plain, practical. Those are *excellent* qualities; and my prayer, therefore, is that many a questioning heart, chancing on these pages, may find a surprisingly lucid and satisfying answer.

J. SIDLOW BAXTER

TABLE OF CONTENTS

Foreword by J. Sidlow Baxter

How Can
I Live
Effectively?

Is God concerned with the details of my life? . . . How does God reveal His will? . . . How important is the will of God? . . . Does the will of God always mean happiness? . . . What if I disagree with the will of God? . . . How can I be certain I'm in the will of God? . . . Does God really have a plan for my life? . . . What if I miss the perfect will of God? Does God have an alternative? . . . How do I go about determining the will of God?

1 HOW CAN I FIND GOD'S WILL FOR MY LIFE?

William Beebe, the naturalist, was a good friend of Theodore Roosevelt. Often after an evening's talk the two men would go out, look up at the sky, and see who could first detect the faint light-mist of the Spiral Galaxy in Andromeda. Then Beebe would say, "That is one of the hundred million galaxies. It is 750,000 light-years away. It consists of one hundred billion suns, each larger than our sun." Whereupon the other would respond, "Now I think we are small enough. Let's go to bed."

I suppose the reason we wonder whether God is interested in "little me" is because everything in our world is so big. The astronomer probes the recesses of space by means of a telescope — the emphasis is on the gigantic. If an astronomer were to tell me that the nearest star to earth is 25 million miles away, I would find it difficult to grasp. Instead, they tell me it is 25 billion miles away — a distance that is almost inconceivable.

If I were to drive my car 100 miles per hour, I would be driving too fast. Yet, when we fly, we often travel more than 600 miles per hour ground speed by jet. On the other hand, we read that the astronauts flew around the world at a clip of 17,000 miles per hour. They watched the sun rise and set every 90 minutes!

The more we think how big this universe is, the smaller we become. We begin to see ourselves as just tiny specks sharing this earth with three billion other specks. Then we wonder: How can such an inconceivably big Creator be interested in something as small as the details of our lives? Can He really be concerned about what we do?

When we think in this fashion we are forgetting one thing. God's concern is not measured by size. The scientists tell us that the atom is as perfectly designed as the star. Everything that God has made is perfectly designed and ordered, whether we are considering the planetary system or a leaf on the elm tree in our front yard.

You might think a man insignificant when compared with a star, but when the two are viewed by our heavenly Father, the star must melt into insignificance. You and I are more important to God than all the merely material parts of His creation. The Bible tells us that man is the crown of all God's earthly creation. Man is unique and superior because he has the power of reason. He can think; he can freely choose and act; he has the ability to love. He is important to God because he is capable of fellowship with Him. He can respond to his Heavenly Father.

Therefore, just as we find design and planning in all of creation, so, even more, God has a plan for each individual human life. God has a plan for you.

Life is full of decisions, and decisions have a way of bringing a time of crisis in our lives. This is especially true if we love God and desire in all our ways to acknowledge Him.

When the final results of our sermon poll were tabulated, there were only a few votes between the top two subjects: "Where are we in Bible prophecy?" and, "How can I know the will of God for my life?"

I am not sure if there is any significant reason for this. It could be that the turmoil of our times and a strong desire to be found in the perfect will of God have a parallel. I cannot speak, of course, for those thousands of laymen who expressed themselves by a vote, but I can speak for myself.

When one feels that time is running out, there is a sense of urgency to do God's will. This is true in my own life, and I have noticed the increased number of inquiries through counseling, correspondence, and calls on our daily broadcast in regard to this very theme. Most of the questions can be wrapped up in one of the following:

DOES GOD HAVE A PLAN FOR MY LIFE?

Remarkably evident in the realm of nature is the care of God for His creation. I was fascinated by a story in the *Reader's Digest* describing the wonder of the Monarch butterflies. These tiny, fragile members of God's creation, weighing little more than a bird's feather, fly hundreds of miles to spend the winter in warmer climates. The flocks of butterflies that span the North American continent and arrive in late October at Pacific Grove, California, have long been famous. An estimated two million Monarchs spend the winter, year after year, on the same trees in a six-acre area.

The most spectacular feature of their migration is that they gather on these same trees each year. Their life span is so short, no butterfly could possibly make the round trip twice. How then, without leader or guideposts, do these tiny wayfarers find their way over such great distances? There is only one answer: God has provided compass and direction for even such frail creatures as the butterfly.

Another demonstration of Divine planning is the eel. These lowly fish come from all over the world to the Gulf Stream off Bermuda to breed. In autumn, when they are ready to lay their eggs, they swim out from the fresh-water streams into the ocean, and from all the rivers of the world they come to this one spot. Having given birth to their young, they die, and in the spring the new-born eels go back to the same river from whence their mothers came.

We can clearly see God's vivid scheme in nature. The silky fine texture of the garment of the lily, the ability of the mocking bird and the canary to sing without voice lessons, the butterfly's returning to its original habitat without compass or map — all are mute evidence of a design by Divine intelligence.

Can we watch the seasons come and go, bringing sunshine, snow, cold, and heat, without marvelling at God's design? When we see a handful of tiny seeds, nurtured by the rich earth, spring forth as crops to feed hungry mouths, we cannot help but breathe a prayer of thanksgiving for God's marvelous handiwork.

Neither can we long consider the intricate workings of the human mind, its capabilities, its intellectual powers, its emotional depths, without noting an intricate plan.

Everywhere we look we see design and order. Does not this necessitate a designer? Now, I ask you: Why would God stop there? The same God who created the butterfly with such care created you and me, and He created us for a purpose.

For six thousand years God has been dealing with man, revealing His purpose and design as clearly as He has revealed it in the material world. In fact, one soon discovers that when man has sought and followed God's will he has prospered; when he has done otherwise he has floundered and suffered. Remember how God directed the lives of men like Joseph and Gideon and Paul? God is Intelligence! Nature proves it. Universal order demonstrates it. His dealings with man declare it.

For my thoughts are not your thoughts, neither are your ways my ways, saith Jehovah. For as the heavens are higher than the earth, so are my ways higher than your ways, and my thoughts than your thoughts (Isaiah 55:8-9).

He will feed his flock like a shepherd, he will gather the lambs in his arm, and carry them in his bosom, and will gently lead those that have their young. Who hath measured the waters in the hollow of his hand, and meted out heaven with the span, and comprehended the dust of the earth in a measure, and weighed the mountains in scales, and the hills in a balance? (Isaiah 40:11-12).

Oh give thanks unto Jehovah . . . who alone doeth great wonders; . . . to Him that smote Egypt in their first-born; . . . and brought out Israel from among them with a strong hand and with an out-stretched arm; . . . that divided the Red Sea in sunder . . . and made Israel to pass through the midst of it; but overthrew Pharaoh and his host in the Red Sea and led his people through the wilderness (Psalm 136).

And thou didst divide the sea before them, so that they went through the midst of the sea on the dry land; . . . Moreover in a pillar of cloud thou leddest them by day; and in a pillar of fire by night, to give them light in the way wherein they should go. Thou camest down also upon Mount Sinai, and spakest with them from heaven, . . . and gavest them bread from heaven for their hunger and broughtest forth water for them out of the rock (Nehemiah 9:11-15).

To all of you who are wondering: Does God have a plan? I answer, Yes, without a doubt!

Is It Important That I Know God's Plan?

When God made man, He made him in His own likeness. The part of us that is specially God-like is our intellect, our free-will or power of choice, and our capacity to love. We are told that we have seven major, positive emotions — desire, faith, love, sex, enthusiasm, romance, and hope. Because of man's disobedience, these characteristics and emotions have become perverted and distorted, but when we are regenerated by God's grace and become His, we are new creatures. "Old things are passed away . . . all things are become new" (II Corinthians 5:17).

"Even so reckon ye also yourselves to be dead unto sin, but alive unto God in Christ Jesus" (Romans 6:11).

This means a lot more than being saved from the sin of Adam's race. With the barrier of sin removed, we can have communion and fellowship with God. As a result of this fellowship and communion, the desire of our heart is to know Him and to do His will.

Paul reminds us, "Ye are not your own; for ye were bought with a price: therefore glorify God" (I Corinthians 6:19-20). It was a moral question Paul was dealing with then, and he was reminding them that the body as well as the soul belongs to God. This is true also of our will, our intellect, our strength, and our devotion.

"What is His plan for me?" is generally one of the first questions a Christian asks. This was true of the Apostle Paul. When he was converted, in that dramatic experience on the Damascus Road, he first asked: "Who art thou, Lord?" And the answer came: "I am Jesus." Then the question: "What wilt thou have me to do?"

Nothing else is so important to the child of God as finding the answer to this same question: "What wilt thou have me to do?"

How Then Can I Determine God's Will?

Out of our ability to love, desire is born. In the very soul of man there is the instinct of affection. Every man has a degree of love because every man has been created in God's image, and God is love. It is from this center of affection that our desires, emotions, and feelings originate. It is impossible for one to be completely loveless, and therefore impossible to be without desire. We do what we do because we desire or want to.

Looking back upon my call into the ministry, there was no audible voice, vision, or dream — and there had never been a preacher in our family — but following my conversion I had a burning desire to help others. This desire came as a result of a new affection. My new love for my Saviour produced new desires, and these desires led me into the full-time ministry.

Our compulsions, our drives, our urges, our passions, our instincts, our appetites, our emotions, our feelings, our prayers begin in the inner man. Man is more than a body. He is a soul. Before a man is converted, he is filled with a guilt complex because of sin. Sin affects his affections, his inner man, and therefore affects his desires. Conversion brings a change in the inner man, consequently affecting his desires, and this in return changes his conduct. Jesus always starts at the center of man's being. He requires that a man repent, which brings about a change where a man really lives.

A news reporter once asked John Kennedy why he wanted to be the President of the United States, and he answered, "Because as President I can best serve my generation." Paul the Apostle stated that his earnest prayer (desire) was for Israel to be saved. He also wrote to the Ephesians, "For this cause I Paul, the prisoner of Christ Jesus in behalf of you Gentiles" (Ephesians 3:1). You see in each of these statements that the action and conduct of the life was a result of the inward desire.

It seems to me that we can best find God's will by seeking to answer seven simple questions:

1. *How much do you love God?*

This is the starting point. We learn to love God by directing our attention toward Him and becoming acquainted with Him, by believing in His power and His concern for us. Jesus said, "Thou shalt love the Lord thy God with all thy heart, and with all thy soul, and with all thy mind, and with all thy strength . . ." (Mark 12:30). David said, "As the hart panteth after the water brooks, so panteth my soul after thee, O God" (Psalm 42:1).

Since we all have an ability to love, we must direct our love toward God. We do this through worship. Worship means worth. Webster defines worship as "reverence that is paid to worth." It suggests an attitude of life, a recognition of God's superiority, and submission to His throne. In our worship we acknowledge His sufficiency and our utter dependence upon Him.

> Sing unto the Lord a new song . . . for the Lord is great and greatly to be praised. The Lord made the heavens. Honor and majesty are before him: strength and beauty are in his sanctuary . . . give unto the Lord the glory due his name (Psalm 96).

Worship includes adoration, which is a term of endearment. It is giving our love to God. Someone has said, "Worship without love is like a flame without heat." Worship is serving, obeying, and loving. Therefore, we direct our love toward Him by worshiping, by honoring, by magnifying, by acknowledging Him as the Creator and the Lord and Saviour of mankind.

We love Him not only for what He is, but also for the fact that He is willing to make known His ways to us. The Psalmist, expressing appreciation to God for all His benefits, included this great fact:

> Bless the Lord, O my soul; and forget not all his benefits: . . . He made known his ways unto Moses, his acts unto the children of Israel (Psalm 103:2, 7).

2. *What about your desires?*

Out of our love a desire is born to know Him and to do His will. Love releases desires, emotions, feelings. Action follows. Love always expresses itself. The Apostle Peter says, "Whom having not seen, ye love . . . yet believing, ye rejoice greatly with joy unspeakable" (I Peter 1:8).

What are your desires? Take time to analyze and to allow the searchlight to be turned upon your innermost feelings. Be honest with yourself. What do you want in life more than anything else? Our Lord told us, "What things soever ye desire, when ye pray, believe that ye receive them, and ye shall have them" (Mark 11:24). Hebrews records the fact that "faith is the substance of things hoped for." What "things" do you *desire*? You say, perhaps, that you are not interested in analyzing your wishes, but in knowing what God desires for your life. Yet before we know God's desire for us, it is well for us to determine our own desires, for often His desires and ours are the same.

> Delight thyself also in the Lord; and He will give thee the desires of thy heart (Psalm 37:4).
>
> Lord, all my desire is before thee; and my groaning is not hid from thee (Psalm 38:9).
>
> He will fulfill the desire of them that fear him: He also will hear their cry (Psalm 145:19).
>
> Brethren, my heart's desire and prayer to God for Israel is, that they might be saved (Romans 10:1).

My wife and I were invited to have lunch with an executive of a large chain of department stores who wanted to find God's will for his life. He had been given an opportunity to enter full-time service for the Lord. It required that he move to another state, and he was seeking counsel as to whether it was the right thing to do. I remember asking him what he really wanted to do. I felt sure that his desire was born out of a sincere love for God. He told me he wanted to work full-time for the Lord, but not necessarily in that particular state. (He told me later that at first he rejected my simple approach to the subject — he wanted a more spiritual answer.)

I pointed out that God often gives to us the desires of our heart and that the starting point is to come to grips with our own true desires. Are they worthwhile? If fulfilled, will they make us better persons? Will they bring glory to God?

How strong is your desire? Is it only a passing wish — or is it born out of love?

3. *Are you willing to do His will?*

George Mueller said, "Nine-tenths of the difficulty is overcome when our hearts are ready to do the Lord's will, whatever it may be. The difficulty arises when we ask God to reveal His will before we are ready to do it unreservedly."

I suggested to our executive friend that he look the position over, picture himself living there and doing the work, and seeing the results of his effort. I suggested that, although he wasn't excited about living in that particular place, he tell God that his desire to work full-time for Him was so great that he would live any place just to be in His service. God wants a willing heart.

We each have a will of our own — in this we are God-like. God will not invade our wills, but waits for us voluntarily to surrender our wills to His. We must bring our will-power into play; and this, of course, includes being willing to pay any price necessary to do His will. Sometimes we have to give up something to gain something of greater value.

Daniel was a young man in Babylon, but he purposed (desired) in his heart not to defile himself with the king's meat or drink. This he desired because he feared God, and he purposed to do God's will regardless of the cost. The same was true with Moses. He chose rather to share ill treatment with the people of God, than to enjoy the "pleasures of sin for a season" (Hebrews 11:25). Notice that it was Moses who was willing! Will-power comes out of desire and affection, and self-denial is often closely associated.

There is a profound truth in John 7:17, one of the greatest statements that came from the lips of Jesus. He said, "If any man willeth to do His will, he shall know of the teaching, whether it is of God, or whether I speak of myself." In other words, if any man is willing to do God's will, he shall know. "He shall know" means that this man shall have illuminated to him the ability to recognize God's plan for his life. "Any man" includes you and me. It does not say a select few or a certain type of person; there are no exceptions.

When you give your will to God and ask Him to make your will His will, you are well on your way to finding His will.

4. *Have you checked with His Word?*

David said, "Thy Word is a lamp unto my feet, and a light unto my path" (Psalm 119:105). God's Word reveals God's will in many matters. If anything is according to His will, it cannot be contrary to His Word. If the Scriptures say "No," then that is final. "Forever, O Jehovah, thy word is settled in heaven" (Psalm 119:89). Jesus said, "Heaven and earth shall pass away, but my words shall not pass away" (Matthew 24:35).

We have in this country a Bureau of Standards guaranteeing uniform systems of measurement — sixteen ounces to a pound, thirty-six inches to a yard, et cetera. God also has a standard, and it is recorded for our instruction in His immutable Word. We are admonished: "Give diligence to present thyself approved unto God, a workman that needeth not to be ashamed, handling aright the word of truth" (II Timothy 2:15).

Read God's Word — slowly and quietly — and listen for His message in your inner heart. Develop a love for His Word. (Your appetite for God's Word indicates how deep your love is.) Be always willing to obey its instructions, for the true test of seeking His guidance is keeping His commandments.

> He that hath my commandments, and keepeth them, he it is that loveth me: and he that loveth me shall be loved of my Father, and I will love him, and will manifest myself unto him (John 14:21).
> For this is the love of God, that we keep his commandments: and his commandments are not grievous (I John 5:3).

Paul prayed that the saints of Colosse "be filled with the knowledge of his will in all spiritual wisdom and understanding" (Colossians 1:9). To the Ephesians he said, "Be ye not foolish, but understand what the will of the Lord is" (Ephesians 5:17). This understanding of the will of God comes through knowing the Word and being obedient to it.

5. Have you earnestly prayed?

Rest quietly before God in prayer. Tell Him about your desires and ask Him to show you why you desire thus and thus. Is it born of the Spirit? Does it spring from love or from selfishness? Is it because you want to do His will, or because of an ulterior motive?

Jesus calls Himself the good Shepherd in John 10. He tells us of the sheep who learn to know and follow the voice of their shepherd, and that if a stranger comes and calls to them, they will not follow. Jesus said, "I am the door of the sheep . . . by me if any man enter in, he shall be saved, and shall go in and out and shall find pasture . . . I am the good Shepherd; and I know mine own, and mine own know me." There is no limit to what we can learn by asking and listening. Decisions should be reached after searching the heart to eliminate wrong motives and prejudices.

In prayer we can best determine why we desire certain things, and prayer should always precede our own judgment. Decisions made in quiet time before the Lord have a way of being the right decisions.

6. *Have you considered the circumstances?*

Many of us can testify that circumstances have changed our lives. The good experiences, as well as the bad, have helped to direct us into God's will. We have proved the truth of Paul's counsel: "And we know that to them that love God all things work together for good, even to them that are called according to his purpose" (Romans 8:28).

Where is there an open door? Where is the need greatest? Where can your talents best be used?

A young man came to see me about full-time service. He expressed his love for God and his desire to make his life count, but he was filled with questions — how? when? where? I asked him about his talents, and he said that this, basically, was his problem. His talent and training were in the field of data processing. How could this be used for the Lord?

Shortly after this interview he saw an advertisement concerning a nationally-known evangelist who used data processing, and it was from this that God led him, step by step, into full-time service. He looked for a need; he weighed his talents; and he found an open door.

We must consider the circumstances in ascertaining God's will. He generally calls us to do what we have the ability to do. He does not trouble us by calling us to do something of which we are not capable, but He expects us to be guided by the talents He has given us.

Allow the circumstances — whether failure or success, an open door or a God-given talent — to lead you into God's perfect will.

7. *Consult your reasoning power.*

"Come now, and let us reason together" (Isaiah 1:18).

In times past God has revealed His Word through visions, dreams, and other supernatural revelations. While God is forever the same and is able to employ any method of His own choosing, we often find the answer we are seeking through our own reasoning. Doesn't He expect us to use the intellect He has given us to find our place in life? We link, by faith, our mind with the great Intelligence of the universe.

Sometimes God guides through the conscience, and at other times through consecrated judgment. Jesus appears to have acted at times by the impelling force affecting His conscience and at other times as a result of sound judgment.

Some people feel that when we become Christians we lay aside our minds and no longer need to do any thinking but rely only upon the heart with its emotions and feelings. Nothing is further from the truth. As we direct our love to Him and bend our wills, making them subservient to His will, as our desires are determined and scrutinized through prayer and the reading of His Word, as we consider the need and our talents, we then, through the intellectual process of thinking, discipline our minds to be receptive to what is the will of God.

Ask yourself these seven simple questions, and the inner voice of the Holy Spirit will guide you into all truth. Man was not fashioned to live by his own design and planning, but under God's control. Place yourself humbly at His feet. Resolve, out of love, to be His servant; live in obedience to His divine Word; and yours will be a useful life.

When you have determined the will of God for your life, you can be certain that it is your highest calling. Spurgeon said, "If God has called you to be a missionary, I would hate to see you shrivel down to be a king."

WHAT IF I HAVE MISSED HIS WILL FOR MY LIFE?

There is a daily assurance that comes to the one who walks in the will of God — the knowledge that God is pleased. Just as He guides you in finding His will, so He will guide you day by day, hour by hour. It is one thing to find God's will; it is another thing to stay in it.

Life is like a ship. It must first have a destination in view and then start for that distant shore. If fear of the storm or of losing its way keeps it always in the harbor, it is of little value. That is one reason it must have a rudder, to be guided continually until its destination is reached.

Of course, human error is possible in finding God's will; but start with the first step, and then trust the Holy Spirit to continue indicating the course that you are to follow. Paul wanted very much to go to Asia but was forbidden of the Holy Spirit, and was redirected.

Now, if you have missed the way, start again by asking yourself the above questions. God loves you and is just as interested in you as ever. Evaluate and see where you missed the way, and learn from your mistakes; then press on and do His will. We sometimes learn as much from our mistakes as from our successes. Just because one has failed, it does not make him a failure.

Finding God's will for your life is not something you do once, and then it's all over. Doing the will of God requires dependence upon Him daily for guidance and direction.

Is there a formula for a happy home? . . . Why are some people who are Christians hard to get along with? . . . Why is there so much friction in the American home today? . . . What can I do about a jealous husband? . . . Are all the rights of married life on the side of the husband? . . . To what extent must the wife be submissive to her husband? . . . Do you believe parents are at fault for delinquency among young people today? . . . What do you feel are the greatest needs in our homes today? . . . Can a person be truly consecrated and live a normal life? . . . Does the Bible give a standard for the conduct of individual family members? . . .

2 WHAT IS THE FORMULA FOR A HAPPY HOME LIFE?

The story is told that during the administration of confirmation to a class about to enter the church, a young girl was asked: what is matrimony? Making a face she said, "Oh, matrimony is a state of terrible torment which those who enter are compelled to undergo for a time to fit them for heaven."

"Oh, no," said the young priest who was helping with the Confirmation class, "you have given the definition of purgatory. It is matrimony we are talking about."

"Let her alone," said the Archbishop. "What do we know about it? Maybe she is right."

Whether the home is purgatory or paradise depends upon the attitudes of the people within that home. A happy home is a blessing not only to the family itself, but to the world. Because of the increasing pressures and influences which have a tendency to destroy the foundations of our homes, we need more than ever to draw tighter the ties that bind us together. Unhappy homes not only lead husbands and wives to divorce court, they also have a demoralizing effect upon the children. Constant tension between parents results in the children forming a distorted view of what home life should be.

Through the years man has been extremely successful in conquering everything but himself. Electricity has been harnessed and made to be man's servant; the water and air no longer limit his activities; and he has made the natural products of the earth the base for his buildings and construction. Inanimate matter has been conquered; but man's insuperable problem is a proper adjustment to himself and his fellowmen.

Young folks spend thousands of dollars a year on education, attending colleges and special schools to gain knowledge and develop skills in their chosen fields. When they finally enter the business world they keep their lessons in mind, for they know that unsatisfactory performance means losing their jobs, and they don't want to be tagged "a failure."

21

The same youth, who spend years preparing for their careers and ardently adhere to certain business practices, fall in love and repeat the marriage vows. With little or no preparation for marriage or consideration of what marriage is, they expect married and family life to run its course automatically, and with it a lifetime of happiness.

People fail to realize that one does not so much "fall in love" as learn to love. Learning to live together harmoniously and happily requires a great deal of understanding, patience, kindness and a forgiving spirit.

There is frequent disagreement in our world. We seem to have an infinite capacity to disagree. Reading the daily newspaper, the one item that overshadows all others is disagreement. The Jews and the Arabs disagree. The Chinese on the mainland and the nationalists of Taiwan disagree. The Hindus dislike the Moslems in India. The different races are clashing in the streets of our own American cities. Capital and labor are at odds with each other. It affects the places where we work, perhaps our schools, and certainly the roots reach into our homes.

Naturally, this business of living together happily and harmoniously is a difficult pursuit. We each have our own peculiarities, our different backgrounds, our own individual disposition and temper. As a result, problems do arise when we rub elbows with one another.

We must admit, however, that it is man's individuality which has made the world an interesting and challenging place to live. But we must remember that God did not create each man uniquely to cause discord and conflict. He created man uniquely so each could contribute his "specialty" to the whole good and happiness of mankind. Unless tolerance and understanding are exercised, the individual uniqueness with which God fashioned us, can cause manifold problems in our society.

This is especially true in marriage and the home situation. Unless each partner in a marriage is mature enough to understand and accept the other's individuality, including different views and actions, much unhappiness can result. Even though a couple may share many mutual interests and opinions, differences are sure to exist. When we become tolerant enough to accept individual differences, we find ourselves enjoying life more, and we avoid much unnecessary conflict.

One cannot hope to understand others until he first defines his own motives, actions, and reactions. Analyzing oneself may well be the largest single step in solving family difficulties. When an individual perceives, not only his strengths, but his weaknesses, and accepts his aptitudes as well as his limitations, he can then work toward self-improvement. Remember, it takes two to disagree. Sometimes what you husbands call the wife's nagging may really be the verbalization of your own shortcomings. Other family members probably see you more objectively than you see yourself. Maybe you *do* have a tendency to be sloppy. Think about it. Perhaps then you won't leave your clothes where you stepped out of them, or the newspaper scattered freely in front of your favorite chair.

Maybe you wives *do* have difficulty budgeting the family income. If you would admit this to yourself and your husband and ask him to supervise the family spending, it could eliminate an overdrawn checking account and avoid family quarrels. And, children, your attention the first time your parents ask you to do or not to do something could eliminate the unnecessary "harping."

When we have stopped long enough to define our motives, our actions, and even our reactions, we can then begin to determine the necessary steps to remove the problems that exist in our homes.

1. Learn to Understand One Another

When you understand someone, you accept him for what he is, and you don't try to remodel him to fit your image of an ideal husband or wife, son or daughter. Now, don't misunderstand me. I am not saying that we cannot help each other to change. But change, the weeding out of each other's bad points, is the result of patience, love, and understanding — not conflict. Elsie Robinson, the journalist, was asked about the possibilities of having a happy marriage. "Practically nil," she said, "unless you want to work at it as the greatest job of your life and not one you will desert when you get your hair rumpled."

Learning to understand one another goes a long way toward finding the solution to our problems at home. There are too many iron curtains within the family circle. We really don't know one another! An Italian proverb says, "Clear understandings develop long friendships." And happy homes develop strong friendships, too. In fact, one of the reasons we have families is to share concern for one another. This is almost impossible without learning to understand each other.

You know, of course, the one problem the minister encounters above all others in counseling is the one of getting along with others. Dr. Richard J. Kremler, an authority on the psychology of marriage and family relationships, said that important factors contributing to the increase of marital problems are loss of understanding between marriage partners, loss of determination to stay married, and unreasonable expectations. "It is clear that increasingly more Americans have marriage problems," Dr. Kremler said.

We can learn to understand each other. I believe our understanding will improve if we learn to . . .

Bear and Forbear

I have often suggested to young couples about to exchange the vows of marriage at the altar that they give birth immediately to a set of twins called "Bear" and "Forbear." At times it has been necessary to give the same advice to gray-haired grandparents. We are constantly discovering things about each other that we never expected, and we must be willing to bear these things and be tolerant one with the other. Benjamin Franklin gave some sound advice when he said, "Keep your eyes wide open before marriage and then half shut afterwards." Emerson cautioned, "Never try to make another individual into a copy of yourself, for God knows, and you should too, that one person like you is all the world can stand."

"To bear" means to be willing to support, to uphold, to sustain. To "forbear" is to refrain and hold back. Both are needed to maintain harmony in the home. It is through sacrifices and concessions made in the right attitude that understanding is created and love is made to grow. It is when we are gladly willing to do what the other person wants to do that we are melted together.

How desperately we need to have tolerance these days! We need to have respect for the beliefs of others even though we think our own are right and best. Having respect for the other person and his beliefs and liberties has made our country great. The same spirit must prevail in the home. We must realize that the other person has a right to his opinions and does not necessarily have to think in every detail as we think. Others have not only a right to their opinion, but should have the right to express it.

One lady said concerning her husband, "I want him to have his opinions — I just don't want to hear them."

Perhaps one of our problems is that we have too many dictators in our homes. Big shots! They think they are right and nobody else is right. Someone asked a woman why there was no lodge meeting that night, and she answered, "It is because the grand, all-powerful, invincible, supreme, omnipotent potentate got beat up by his wife — that's why there is no lodge meeting tonight!"

In our day when there is so much friction, and so many things are almost unbearable, if we would learn to get along with each other in the home, we must learn to bear as well as forbear.

Don't Major on Minors

When you see a fault in another member of the family, be very careful about calling it to his attention. Instead, seek for understanding. It is wise to ask yourself: Why does he act this way? Instead of criticism, you might find the cause and be able to help.

We react certain ways when we are tired or when our pride is hurt. If one is alone too much or experiences a time of sorrow, it affects his outlook. So don't harp on the other person's faults — be considerate. Accept him as he is — with all his virtues and his faults.

One of the opportunities in marriage is to mature and grow, and the greatest benefit results when right attitudes are maintained toward each other. One of the fruits of love is the ability to overlook faults. "Love is kind . . . thinketh no evil; rejoiceth not in iniquity, but rejoiceth in the truth" (I Corinthians 13:4-6). Someone remarked, "Home is where you are treated the best but you grumble the most." It should not be so. It should be "Where a world of strife is shut out and a world of love is shut in."

I like the advice of the family counselor who said, "Never shout in the home unless the house is on fire. When there is much shouting in the home, that home actually is on fire — love is going up in smoke."

Dwelling on the negatives not only destroys sacred relationships but often embitters lives. Henry Ward Beecher said he received a letter that contained only one word: "Fool." Telling his congregation about it, he remarked, "I've received many anonymous letters, but this is the most unique one I ever received. The anonymous writer signed his name, 'Fool,' but failed to enclose the letter!"

One is a fool who continues to major on the negatives and minor faults when majoring on the positives produces far more beautiful music. The next time you are tempted to quarrel ask yourself: Is this really important? Remember, no one has ever gained anything from an argument, but you always lose something. Why hurt someone just to show you are right? There are no good quarrels! So remember, don't major on the minors.

Share Responsibility

Sharing our love always creates a song in the soul and brings harmony in the family as well. Learning to share the duties and responsibilities of the home and family is of utmost importance. I suppose if we could exchange places, putting ourselves in the position of another, we would better understand each other. If my wife could be the preacher and the pastor for just 30 days, she would better understand why I say and do as I do. If I were able to do her work for the same length of time, then I would better understand and perhaps would feel differently about the endless chores of the parsonage.

There is no such thing as a self-made man. Without the influence of our parents, our school teachers, and others, we would be almost worthless. The same is true in the home. No one can build a happy home alone; a sense of mutual responsibility is necessary to maintain a good understanding. We can even share the responsibility of overcoming the habit of quarreling.

I read that one young couple who were having a lot of friction between them decided that they would work together and overcome the problem of quarreling. Since they lived on a farm, the husband reminded the wife that sometimes things go wrong with the livestock and the machinery, and he said, "If you see me coming into the house with my cap pulled way down low, you will know that I need help, so be extra kind and loving." She promised she would, but then she reminded him that things don't always go right in the house — the cream won't churn; the fire won't burn; the stove won't bake right; and meals are late. She said, "When that happens, I am all upset, and those are the days when I need a lot of love and a lot of patience from you. So when you come to the house and see my apron tied up high, you will know that I need special consideration."

Everything went fine. Once in awhile John would come in with his cap way down, and Mary would be very affectionate and understanding. And sometimes he would return from the field when Mary had the apron tied high, so he would say sweet words that every woman loves to hear. But one day he came in, and the cap was down; he took one look at Mary, and the apron was tied high. What do you think happened? They just had to laugh at each other! There was no quarreling that day. You see, sharing responsibility helps create understanding between us.

2. Maintain Communication

Essential to understanding members of our families is the ability to carry on free and relaxed conversation. Some people say that "silence is golden," but too often the lack of communication between family members forms a roadblock to happiness. Misunderstandings, suspicions, quarreling, and often a family break-up are direct results of the lack of communication.

The more I work with people the more I realize that communication is vital to marital happiness and family harmony. It is the basis of all understanding. Family members owe it to one another to encourage free and relaxed conversation. This is done, not through arguing, but through discussion. Discussion not only relieves tension and avoids harsh and unpleasant words; it also is a method of thinking together. When domestic situations are discussed by the family, understanding is developed; right attitudes and changes of behavior are born.

Mature marriage partners undoubtedly realize that disagreements are sure to arise but should not be allowed to grow into lengthy quarrels. The Apostle Paul gives some advice which all family members would be wise to remember. He suggests that all difficulties be settled on the same day they arise — before nightfall. "Let not the sun go down upon your wrath" (Ephesians 4:26).

An eighteen year old girl told her pastor that her parents hadn't spoken to each other for years. Their only communication was note-writing, the notes being delivered by the children. If they were in a situation where they had to say something to each other, the dad said it to a child, who repeated it to the mother. The mother gave her reply in similar fashion through a child. This had been going on for years. Can you imagine the unhappiness of the children in that home? The pastor asked the girl the obvious question: "When did this get started?" She replied, "It started years ago when Mom and Dad couldn't agree on having the neighbors over for dinner."

There are a few things I have noticed that help keep the lines of communication open.

Show Appreciation Toward Each Other

Dr. George Crans said, "Appreciative words are the most powerful force for good will on earth." If only we could take time and thought to let one another know how we appreciate what others do for us! The cardinal calamity is when we begin to take people within the home for granted. A smile, a kiss, a little candy or flowers on a birthday or anniversary, go a long way to build communications. But don't feel it has to be some special day or big "happening" to be kind or show appreciation. Express it about little things. Their work, their faithfulness, or just being able to tolerate living with you. Those who do housework and care for the children, it seems to me, especially deserve our appreciation. When I think of the endless duties of cleaning house, cooking a hundred thousand meals during a lifetime, serving as nurse through the mumps, chicken pox and measles; helping the children with homework, plus laundry and ironing (with no extra pay — and often with no words of appreciation) it makes me ashamed that I haven't been more thoughtful.

A gentleman noticed a lady with ten children getting on the bus, and he asked: "Are these yours, or are you going on a picnic?" She answered, "They're mine — and it's no picnic!"

There are many daily tasks performed by those around us that are "no picnic," but become bearable when appreciation is expressed. I have had many men tell me they have never heard their wives express appreciation for the long hours of labor in their businesses. This is true in spite of the fact that the Scriptures teach that wives are to "submit themselves to their husbands, as unto the Lord" (Ephesians 5:22). This word "submit" means to yield one's person to the power of another. His will, his ambitions, his dreams become hers, and in that way her sincere appreciation toward her husband becomes a vital part in making a happy home.

In the account of creation, God took a rib from Adam, and from the rib ". . . made he a woman" (Genesis 2:23). I think it is noteworthy that she was not out of the man's head, to dominate him, nor out of his feet to be trampled upon by him, but out of his side that she might be equal with him, from under his arm to be protected by him, and from near his heart to be loved by him.

When the spirit of love and appreciation flows between husband and wife, the children also benefit, for they sense the harmony and are well adjusted for life. In fact, the most important thing a father and mother can do for their children is to love one another.

Develop a Sense of Humor

To see the funny side of things and laugh at our own mistakes helps tremendously to keep the line of communication open. I agree with the preacher who said, "If you could just sit on the fence and watch yourself pass by, you would die laughing at the sight."

The other day was one of those days I thanked God for a sense of humor. As I was preparing to go to the office my younger daughter came in to say that I had to take the dog to the veterinarian on my way to work. Rushed because of the additional chore, I hurriedly put on my shirt and tie. As I adjusted the tie, my shirt split down the back. My wife told me to go ahead and wear it, saying no one would know the difference. But I knew that I had to go to the barber that day, and I would have to take off my coat.

I changed shirts in a hurry, put the tie and cuff links on, collected in one hand the books I had been studying, and with the other grabbed my coat. Starting out the door, I saw a pitcher of grape juice on the kitchen counter and thought I ought to have a drink of that before I went to work. It happened to be one of the frozen concentrates and was not completely melted. When I tipped the pitcher it just went whoosh — all over my face and shirt. Standing there looking at me, my wife said, "And it stains, too."

I laid down the books and coat and ran to get another shirt — but there were no more. I recovered one from the dirty clothes, pressed it, and again got ready to go. I picked up the dog and went to the vet. Walking into the office I failed to see a small step and fell. The dog went one way and I another.

When at last I reached the church, it was three minutes before my daily broadcast which starts at nine o'clock. Having the books and papers in one hand, I tried with my free hand to reach the opposite pocket for my office key. The books dropped, and papers scattered. As I walked into the office the phone was ringing. It was my wife. I told her what had happened and laughingly asked, "Is this Friday the 13th?"

"No," she replied, "that's next Friday!"

You have those days, don't you? Without a sense of humor and the ability to laugh at yourself in life, tensions would mount. Therefore, I believe we need more taffy in life and less epitaphy. By that I mean that we can often break the tensions and improve our communications by learning to laugh at our mistakes. Develop a sense of humor!

Be Willing to Forgive and Forget

An unforgiving spirit and unwillingness to forget have broken communications between many people. Let me tell you a sad story. After church one evening a lady asked if she could have a personal word with me. As we entered my study, she asked if I would perform a marriage for her. She was a woman of middle age, with a few gray hairs, and I asked for a little information before consenting. She then told me this story.

Many years before she had married a man, and they had two sons. Then something happened — nothing major, just a disagreement, a few harsh words, and one thing led to another. They were both stubborn and each continued to harp on his own view of things. Finally, they separated and divorced. Twenty-five years had passed. Neither had remarried. Then one day she learned through a friend that he was in the hospital, and she came to Denver to see him. She came because she thought he might need help. In the passing of the years one of the boys had died, and the other had lost track of his parents. Well, at the hospital she realized what a fool she had been, and she asked forgiveness. He did the same, and they wanted me to come to the hospital and remarry them.

Leaving the hospital room after the ceremony I thought, how sad to have wasted so many years — all because of an unwillingness to forgive and forget.

We are so prone to strain at a gnat and swallow a camel. It is easy to be dogmatic and insist that we are right, but we find it so hard to ask forgiveness. Jesus cautions us, in the parable of the unmerciful servant, about the sin of unforgiveness. He told us in Matthew 6:15, "But if ye forgive not men their trespasses, neither will your Father forgive your trespasses."

I have never met a happy couple who have not learned to forgive and forget. If we maintain communication through appreciation, developing a sense of humor, and being willing to forgive and forget, we have taken some giant steps toward solving the problems at home.

3. LET GOD BUILD THE HOUSE

It takes some doing on God's part to bring about these solutions. Of course, it takes more than brick and mortar to make a home, and no home life can be complete unless God has a part. When our house begins to show deterioration we take steps to make repair. We spend a lot of time maintaining our home and yard and planning the family meals, but let's not overlook that we must also spend some time in spiritual maintenance.

It is recorded in Genesis that Isaac "builded an altar . . . and pitched his tent there" (Genesis 26:25). No house is complete — be it a mansion or a shack — without an altar to God. It is at the family altar that God meets with the family, and the family meets God.

Let us daily ask God to help us within the family circle to understand one another and to maintain communication so that we can bring honor and glory to His name. Spiritual values must be the core of life if we are to live with meaning.

How can I overcome trouble or live above it? . . . What does God require of me? . . . What is the secret of a balanced life? . . . Are Christianity and happiness synonymous? . . . What makes life really worth living? . . . What is the difference between success and failure? . . . What did Jesus say about life? . . . What is the Biblical definition of effective living? . . . Of happiness? . . . How does the Christian measure success? . . . How can I make my mark in life? . . . Is it possible to live without worry? . . . Is it possible to live a worthwhile life? . . . What about the circumstances that always get me down? . . . Can I live a victorious life all the time?

3 HOW CAN I LIVE A FULL AND EFFECTIVE LIFE?

Everyone wants to be happy! And everyone can be happy. Then, of course, we wonder why everyone isn't happy. I think we all feel that to live effectively we must to some degree find happiness. Those of us who read the Bible cannot help but notice the lilting Gospel and the joy of those first-century Christians.

The New Testament opens with Christmas bells, choirs of angels, and a message of good tidings to all people. Yet we see around us a world of heartache, tears, misery, burdens — people running from problem to problem with little meaning to their earthly existence. For many there is a great difference between what life is today and what they had anticipated life would be. In spite of the tug and the tussle and the hard work some are either losing ground or wondering just where this "rat race" will eventually lead.

Life for many seems to be rather hollow and empty — like the little boy's description of salt. He said, "Salt is what spoils the potatoes when you leave it out." Many lives seem to have something missing, and unfortunately, they do not know what.

As I considered the hundreds of questions submitted to me on this subject of life and how to make it worthwhile, I was fascinated by the clear teaching and wisdom of God's Word on this subject. When I first became a pastor twenty years ago I was very conservative in my theology. My preaching was limited to over-sharp distinctions between the "saint" and the "sinner." It was either heaven or hell, sin or salvation. Then I was confronted with all kinds of problems — problems about life and how to live it and how to make it worthwhile. I soon learned that one could be ready for heaven and not necessarily ready for life down here. So I turned to the sacred Scriptures and found them to be a book of life. True, the Bible is a book of eternal life, but it is also a book of wisdom pertaining to this earthly pilgrimage.

There is not one doubt in my heart that God wants everyone of us to live a happy, effective life during the here and now. Let me make at least five suggestions that will help you.

First, we must . . .

LEARN WHAT LIFE REALLY IS

Life is a pilgrimage. Anyone who makes this journey will find not only smooth places, but rough places as well. Life presents to all of us mountain-peak experiences along with occasional valley experiences when we sink into the depths of despair. At times the far horizons can be clearly seen, and at times the fog lingers, and we grope in confusion with visibility almost zero. Everyone learns, sooner or later, that life does not consist of sunshine only — it also has some shadows. We all experience a measure of both.

Everyone has experienced discouragement and personal misfortune. We have all made mistakes. Who of us have not become discontented with ourselves and felt beaten? I read once that a new post office was built in the eastern part of the United States at a cost of three million dollars. When the building was ready for dedication it was discovered that there was no place to mail a letter!

As you read the dramatic stories of the Biblical heroes of faith, you discover that they also had their ups and downs. This is the stuff of which life is made. Life can be both tragic and tremendous. There come hours of grief as well as days of gaiety; times when you tread into the depths of suffering, or into a night of dark difficulty. You will learn to love, and at times to love deeply, only to find that to love deeply means to suffer deeply. One thing for sure . . . at the heart of life are love and suffering.

At times we blame others for our failures, but other times we know they are the result of our own inadequacy. Jesus told us that the storm came to the house built on the rock as well as to the one built on the sand. The Old Testament tells how Joseph was sold by his brothers as a slave for twenty pieces of silver. It is always sad when one brother sells another for a profit. Young Joseph certainly found that life was not all sunshine; yet in spite of the cruel way he had been treated, he determined to be the best slave in all of Egypt.

Then he was tempted to sin with a married woman. He refused. Consequently he went to prison and was forgotten for years! Still, Joseph counted on God, knowing that God had never promised that life should be always free from trouble or heartache. Therefore, he remained faithful to God during those years spent in the prison.

Paul, the great saint of the New Testament, did not escape heavy trials and sufferings. Acts 24 tells how on one occasion the storm was so great that the vessel on which he travelled was dashed to pieces against the rocks. Although perfect and pure, the Lord Jesus one time said, "My soul is very sad and deeply grieved, so that I am almost dying of sorrow" (Matthew 26:37, *Amplified Bible*).

How quickly these moments of tragedy can come! The sky may be blue one moment, then the next there comes a storm — a flash flood, a car wreck, a heart attack — suddenly something happens startlingly unexpected. I counseled with a young man in the father's room of a hospital some months ago. The doctor had just related to him the news that his newborn child was hopelessly deformed. I shall never forget the words this distraught father spoke: "Pastor, we weren't expecting anything like this!" No doubt such situations caused Bruce Barton to write, "Trouble is chronic; it is not an interruption in the normal processes of life; trouble is life."

Thank God, life also has its joys. We experience those wonderful days when our vision is clear, and we concur with Solomon of old who said, "A merry heart doeth good like a medicine" (Proverbs 17:22). We throw our shoulders back and energetically say, "Today I feel terrific!" The horizon is bright; our vision is 20-20; and we know the joy of living.

If we are to make every day really worth living, we must realize that life is a mixture of the pleasant and the painful, and both are real. I do not think a man would be supremely happy if he never had any problems. By that I mean that God has so designed us that we must conquer our environment; we must overcome our circumstances. As a photographic plate is developed in darkness, so it is that we often find happiness in overcoming our circumstances and obstacles.

Whenever a person says to me, "I don't think life is worth living," then I know that one of two things has happened. He has not yet discovered what life is all about — that even the happy life is not all smooth sailing — or he does not have worthwhile goals.

After we have learned what life really is, we must learn to . . .

LIVE ONE DAY AT A TIME

I have noticed many times that people who are having breakdowns — mentally, physically and spiritually — are attempting to live more than one day at a time, trying to live yesterday, today, and tomorrow all the same day.

There are those who constantly live in the past, wrapped up in yesterday's disappointments and mistakes. This is a load one simply cannot carry without complications. Soon one begins to think that the past is the pattern for the future, and that there is not much to look forward to. The disappointments and hurts of yesterday are pretty hard pillows to sleep on, so we do not sleep. As a result, we become more nervous and eventually conclude that life has but little meaning, that existence consists only of worry and monotony. It was perhaps with this in mind that the Psalmist said, "It is vain for you to rise up early, to sit up late, to eat the bread of sorrows: for he giveth his beloved sleep" (Psalm 127:2).

Learn to live one day at a time. Forget the mistakes of yesterday, except to learn from them. And in addition to forgetting the past, learn to forgive yourself. Don't carry around a constant grudge against yourself because you made a mistake yesterday. If someone can build a three-million dollar post office and forget to provide a mail-slot, is it unusual that the rest of us make mistakes? We must forget those things that are behind except to salvage from them the lessons we need to learn.

Someone has said that being licked is valuable if we learn from it. If, on the other hand, all we remember is the licking and not the lesson, it weakens us for future struggles. Spurgeon reminded us that we are prone "to write our failures in brass and our victories in water." To live a full, happy, worthwhile life, don't attempt to carry yesterday's mistakes today. And whatever you do, don't try to live tomorrow today!

I like the thought expressed by D. W. Whittle in a song, "I Have Nothing to Do With Tomorrow."

I have nothing to do with tomorrow;
Its sunlight I never may see,
So today with my plow in the furrow
To my Master I faithful would be.

I have nothing to do with tomorrow;
My Saviour will make that His care
Its grace and its strength I can't borrow,
So why should I borrow its care?

I encounter a number of people who are living on the installment plan as far as happiness is concerned. They have adopted the phrase, "Just as soon as . . ." They say, "Just as soon as I get my education I will be happy . . . Just as soon as I get married I will be happy . . . Just as soon as I get a new job . . ." et cetera. They attribute their unhappiness to unrealized dreams. These people cannot enjoy the happiness of today because of impatience for the expected joys of tomorrow. They are not content because they want to live tomorrow today.

It has been estimated that 40 per cent of all our worries relate to future incidents which never happen; 30 per cent of the things we worry about happened yesterday and cannot be changed by worry. Twelve per cent of our worries concern health difficulties which never occur. Ten per cent are miscellaneous worries without foundation. Add them all together, and it is apparent that only eight per cent of all we worry about will ever happen — and none of the anxieties could be changed by any amount of worry! Yet, many people reach back into the past to bring their mistakes and faults into today and worry about them. At the same time, they cast a shadow over tomorrow by saying, "What if . . .?" They cannot be happy today because they are anxious about what might happen tomorrow. "What if I get sick? . . . What if I lose my job?"

This is why I say, learn to live one day at a time — live today! The Bible says, "*This* is the day which the Lord hath made; we will rejoice and be glad in it" (Psalm 118:24). We are not to be sad and disappointed over yesterday. Nor are we to be concerned for tomorrow's burden.

Light Your Pathway With a Purpose

The mechanics of living are not adequate ends to content the heart of man. He must have a purpose for living. That purpose must be more than a dream. It must become the cause for which he lives.

Life — to be worthwhile — requires heart and soul, and one gives his heart and soul best when life is filled with a specific purpose. John Wanamaker said, "A man is not doing much until the cause he works for possesses all there is of him." The men and women of history who have been influential in leading mankind around some crucial corner have always been those whose lives were controlled by a purpose. Emerson, the great philosopher, once said, "We do not master our ideas, but we allow our ideas to master us." Most of us, whether we recognize it or not, are moving toward some goal. Otherwise we are just lost in life's shuffle, nothing more than derelicts floating helplessly upon the sea of time.

A great deal depends upon our purpose for living. Our Lord told His disciples on one occasion, "For this cause came I unto this hour" (John 12:27). The one compulsion and vision that dominated His every action was to give His life a ransom and be obedient to His heavenly Father. He had a dominating purpose.

Several months ago I began to ask those with whom I was privileged to counsel concerning their purpose in life. I found that nine out of ten had only a vague idea of their goals. Few had really concentrated on what they wanted out of life, and many admitted that they were drifting without a purpose, and as a result were frustrated. Frustration was sapping their energy. To many of these life was like riding a merry-go-round. Each day they would climb on a gilded horse and go round and round, but never get anywhere. And we all know that constant going, but getting nowhere, makes one dizzy. Life to them was monotonous because it had no meaning.

On the other hand I have watched people driven by a strong desire to reach a goal and willing to pay any price to achieve their desired end. Of course, life for them had meaning. As one little lady told me, "The doctors don't know why I am getting well, but I do — I have something to live for."

Sad indeed is the man who has nothing to live for! And the world is full of these people. They get up to go to work, to come home, to eat, to go to bed, to get up to go to work, to come home . . . . The monotony and routine of everyday living has worn them down. They lack the ability to live above their circumstances, because they have nothing worthwhile to live for. They may have a lot to live *with*, but nothing to live *for*, and that nearly always spells trouble. They bring to mind Joan Sizer's "Rag Doll."

I have a rag doll.
Her hair is just yellow yarn,
Her body is soft and stained;
White cotton pokes through
Where her heel is worn.
Her eyes are too round,
And her nose isn't there.
Yellow yarn hair falls
Over her face.
Her Smile is just painted on.
She wears a faded dress
Covered with flowers.
Poor rag doll; she has no aim
Or purpose; she doesn't even
Have a heart. Poor rag doll.
I know a lot of rag dolls.

If you find a nagging desire to run away from life, it is generally due to the lack of a real reason to live.

As I drove out of the church parking lot some months ago I noticed a middle-aged woman weeping as she waited at the bus stop. I drove around the block, parked my car, then came and introduced myself to her as the pastor of the church. When I offered my assistance she was embarrassed and said there was nothing seriously wrong. I explained that when I saw her weeping I thought she might be ill. Then came the surprise, as she answered, "No, I am not ill; I am just bored with everything."

She spoke in broken English, and I stepped a little closer to catch each word. She continued to pour out her heart, telling me about her family of four children and a hard-working husband. "I get up early every morning," she said, "fix breakfast, pack lunches, and then take a bus over here and work as a cleaning woman in one of the homes nearby. Then I wait here each evening for a bus to go home, and I know what is waiting for me when I get there — more work and a few hours of sleep, only to do the same thing again tomorrow. I am not sick — only tired of the same thing day after day."

This story can be repeated many times, not only by those who do housework, but by those who wear white collars as well.

I was seated by a psychiatrist during a recent plane trip, and we struck up a conversation about life in general. After some conversational sharing of experiences, he told me that most of the people he dealt with professionally were unhappy, and stated that from his point of view they were unhappy for three reasons: boredom, worry, and the fact that they were wrapped up in themselves.

So true! People with no reason for living soon become bored. Then when a crisis comes they want to run away. You know the word *crisis* means decisiveness, and sometimes it is easier to run away than to make a decision. But the next time you feel like running, ask yourself: Do I really have a reason to live?

Jesus said, "He that findeth his life shall lose it; and he that loseth his life for my sake shall find it" (Matthew 10:39). If we try to grab everything for ourselves, then we are not going to be happy. Our little boys and girls have the right idea when they sing:

> J-O-Y, J-O-Y, surely shall be seen,
> Jesus first, Yourself last,
> And Others in between.

When I visited South Korea as the guest of the Oriental Missionary Society I was immediately impressed with the growth and outreach of the cause of Christ throughout the country. I remember when I asked Dr. Kilbourne the secret of this advance of Christianity, he told me of the great need that existed in Korea at the end of the war. South Korea was primarily agricultural, and when the division came, much of the industries and wealth were in North Korea. Because they were hungry, many of the Koreans came to the missions for soup and clothing. When they were converted the missionaries instructed them: "Now, as a Christian, go and find the worst cases in your village and share with them." These people, who were themselves nearly naked, found others in greater need and shared with them. As they shared, they forgot their own circumstances and found life worthwhile.

Erich Fromm said, "The deepest need of man is the need to overcome his separateness, to leave the prison of his aloneness. The full answer to the problem of existence lies in true and mature love."

May I challenge you to let your love wrap itself around those you come in contact with each day, and at the end of the day you will say that life has been wonderful.

When Robert Maynard Hutchins was president of the University of Chicago he said, "We do not know where we are going, or why, and we have almost given up the attempt to find out. We are in despair because the keys which were to open the gates of heaven have let us into a larger but more oppressive prison-house. We thought these keys were science and the free intelligence of man. They have failed us. We have long since cast off God. To what can we now appeal?"

Let Christ appeal to you. Let His will be your will. Devote your life to serving Him, and give of yourself to ease the load on someone else's shoulder. Let this be the purpose to lighten your pathway, and I assure you, life will be worthwhile.

Look for God at Every Turn of the Road

There are two philosophies of life, one of which I must endorse. I can choose to believe that I am a plaything of chance. If I believe this, I may as well "eat, drink and be merry, for tomorrow I may die." On the other hand, I can choose to believe that my life is in the hands of God, and that He is interested in all that happens to me. I can believe that He directs my life. In every event that comes to me, I can believe that God has allowed it for a purpose, that He is trying to do something for my good! I choose to believe the latter.

I say this because Romans 8:28 says, "And we know that to them that love God all things work together for good, even to them that are called according to his purpose." It does not say that all things are good for all people. This is not a promise for every Tom, Dick, and Harry. It is for those who have as their purpose in life to love God and be called according to His purpose. Neither does it say that all things work together for good in spite of the way we live. Jesus said, "If you love me, you will keep my commandments" (John 14:15). If, therefore, I love God and my purpose in life is to do His will, then whatever happens, it will work out for the best in my life. Remember, Joseph told his brothers, after their reunion when they were fearful of his vengeance, "Ye meant evil against me, but God meant it for good" (Genesis 50:20).

The person who knows what life is, and lives it one day at a time, can begin to look for God in every situation. How does this make life worthwhile? If I know my life has an eternal purpose, monotony ceases. If I believe that what I do today has an eternal value, that God is unfolding a plan whereby He has allowed each circumstance to come my direction, and that He is making me a better person, then I can learn to rejoice in the night-time even as I rejoice in the sunshine. Then I begin to look for God's plan and His will in everything that happens.

One man said to me, "Pastor, I know I must be out of God's will — my back is against the wall." It is not necessarily so. All Joseph did was dream good dreams and refuse to sin, but he was cast into prison. Remember, life has its shadows as well as its sunshine. It takes the crushing of the rose to bring forth the utmost fragrance. Therefore, I choose to look for God in everything that comes to me. I try to discover what God is endeavoring to work out in my life.

When times of discouragement come, and they surely will, ask God to reveal Himself in that particular experience. There is a reason God has allowed it to happen — so look for that something that He desires to show you.

> Delight yourselves in the Lord; yes, find your joy in him at all times. Have a reputation for gentleness, and never forget the near-

ness of your Lord. Don't worry over anything whatever; tell God every detail of your needs in earnest and thankful prayer, and the peace of God, which transcends human understanding, will keep constant guard over your hearts and minds as they rest in Christ Jesus (Philippians 4:4-7. *Phillips Translation*).

Wait on the Lord; be of good courage, and he shall strengthen thine heart: wait, I say, on the Lord (Psalm 27:14).

The steps of a good man are ordered by the Lord: and he delighteth in his way. Though he fall, he shall not be utterly cast down: for the Lord upholdeth him with his hand (Psalm 37:23-24).

Take strength from these great and sure promises.

When you face discouragement, whether it is sorrow at the loss of a loved one, an unsatisfactory romance, disappointment at the loss of a promotion, or regret because of a personal failure, learn to see God at every turn of the road.

Link Yourself With Divine Power

No life can be at its best without God's help. We must take time to let God renew spiritual life within us. We are so busy. We are always on the go. So many have developed a restlessness — always wanting to be somewhere else. I know it is hard to be still. Yet it is in the quiet hours that God restores our soul and gives us strength for life. It is as we let go and let God that He gives us a sense of worth.

God is life. And God gives us life when we have fellowship with Him. When we break off that fellowship, life begins to die and becomes dull, worthless, and uninteresting. This is why it is necessary to get alone with God in the quiet time and renew that life which only God gives. When it is renewed, life has a purpose. Life has a meaning.

Our worship service each Sunday morning is telecast. Sometime ago a lady and her elderly husband in a neighboring state awoke one Sunday morning with the decision that they might as well turn on the gas and end it all. The husband was paralyzed from the neck down, and the wife had just learned that she had incurable cancer. As the lady got up to turn on the gas, she felt an impulse to turn on the television set. The first words she heard were a part of my message, as I said, "God will help you regardless of the circumstances." This caught their attention, so they listened to the entire broadcast.

A few weeks later this lady wrote to a member of our church and said that as a result of the telecast they had given their lives to God. Linking ourselves with Divine power is a match for any circumstance.

If we are to overcome the weakness within which causes us defeat in our Christian experience, we must link ourselves with God's power. We must turn away from the things that discourage us and look toward God. Regardless of the cause that undermines and defeats us, God's resources are adequate. Having God's power within us, we can confront and defeat whatever circumstance life may send our way.

Do you want a satisfying life, a life without a feeling of emptiness, and different from that purposeless kind of existence which you sometimes seem to live? Such a meaningful life can be found only in fellowship with God — a fellowship which satisfies the immortal spirit within us. When we live near to God, He becomes real; and then life, too, becomes real, healthily exciting and vital.

For a life worthwhile:

> Learn what life really is;
> Live one day at a time;
> Light your pathway with a purpose;
> Look for God at every turn of the road; and
> Link yourself with Divine power.

Is fear a sin? . . . Should Christians ever be afraid? . . . Is fear ever good? . . . How can I overcome the fear of losing my job? . . . What if fear just naturally comes? . . . How can I conquer fear? . . . Did Jesus talk about fear? . . . I am a Christian; yet I am afraid to die. Can we really live above fear? . . . How can I turn fear into trust? . . . Is constant fear an indication that I am not really a Christian? . . . Does God ever cause us to be afraid?

4 HOW CAN I OVERCOME FEAR?

Historians, statesmen, and the well-known news media have already stamped the time in which we are now living as "the scientific age." Undoubtedly, the history of our time has been highlighted by man's spectacular effort to conquer space. We have witnessed vast change in every human endeavor. Perhaps some people think a more characteristic name for this era would be "the aspirin age." More than 28 million pounds of aspirin were sold in America last year. Equally fitting, in fact I believe closer to a true description, would be the name tag, "the age of fear."

Most people today battle this thing called fear. When one takes into consideration that the subject of fear was sixth from the top in our poll, plus the fact that many other questions on different subjects were asked out of fear, one begins to realize the importance of the subject.

A variety of questions were asked, such as: What is fear? . . . Why am I so fearful? . . . Is it wrong or a sin to be afraid? But for the most part those who responded wanted to know how to *overcome* and live above fear. Some wondered if fears were "real," while others asked for help in dealing with a specific fear, such as: "How can I overcome the fear of losing my job?" Many openly admitted that they were fearful about finances, job security, problems of health, not being liked by others, not pleasing God, etc. But what surprised me most were the many who expressed their fears of feeling inadequate to meet the everyday demands of life.

Through these questions I have a better understanding of the feelings and the fears of those around me. As I began to take a personal inventory of my own fears and feelings, I found myself in the same boat, battling the same wearying winds. So with renewed compassion I sought for the answer to these vital questions.

Again, I found God's Word held the answers for which I was seeking. As I turned the pages there was no question in my heart that its words were dependable. It was a message from the Eternal! The words became a lamp unto my feet and a light unto my pathway. Its message came through loud and clear that God thinks a great deal of us. He not only created us in His own image, but has provided salvation for us through the Lord Jesus Christ. He has made it possible for us to be the sons of God — children of light and temples of the Holy Spirit — not creatures of defeat, walking continually in the valley of tormenting fear, but filled with power to live a dynamic life above the shadows of fear.

Yes, fear is real. It affects our minds, our bodies and our spirits. I know some are trying to tell us that fear doesn't really exist, but the Apostle Paul spoke of "fightings within and fears without." Fear is real and is an adversary. It narrows our vision and weakens our resistance and brings frustration. It produces doubt and self-distrust, resentment and sometimes hate. If allowed to fester it becomes destructive. It must be conquered if we are to be our best; for when we are afraid we often make wrong decisions.

Fear is inner panic. It is a feeling of being unable to cope with the problem that confronts us. Fear is the imagination gone wild, the feeling that the worst thing possible is going to happen.

It is often a nameless dread.

But to know that fear is real and what it produces is, within itself, not sufficient. A physician does not stop with diagnosing a malady. That is only the starting point.

There are five significant truths within the Scriptures which will help us to overcome these mental monsters and "cancers of the conscience" called fears.

1. *BE SURE . . . you are right with God*

Fear and sin have always gone hand in hand. The first wages of sin was fear, for Adam said, "I was afraid and I hid myself." Sin and guilt make cowards of us all. We often run because we are afraid. Fearlessness starts with Divine forgiveness. Forgiveness from God always brings confidence.

When the angels announced the birth of Jesus, the first two words were "Fear not." Why? Because they announced the good news of the coming Saviour. "Thou shalt call his name Jesus; for he shall save his people from their sins" (Matthew 1:21). Being saved from sin is the starting point of overcoming fear. Jesus said, "Ye shall know the truth, and the truth shall make you free" (John 8:32). What is the truth that will set us free? It is the knowledge that, although we are sinners, Jesus our Saviour stands ready to forgive.

We may ignore the Saviour, and live as we please, run the business of our lives without asking for Divine help, and behave as if there were no Divine laws and no eternity. We can attempt to repress our fears and frustrations and smother our guilt feelings; or we can throw restraint to the wind and express our desires and do what we want to do any time we want to do it. We can take the attitude, "After all, my life is my own — I can do as I please."

There are many examples of men who took this route. Saul of the Old Testament is one. Few men are endowed with greater advantages than he. He came from a good family. A man of splendid physique, he had a sunny, modest disposition, and was extremely courageous. In spite of the fact that he was called to be king, enjoyed the presence of God, and was surrounded by many wonderful friends, he decided to go his own way. It wasn't long until problems developed and fear came, as it always does, and he sought for help outside of God. Saul ultimately admitted that he had "played the fool"; and he died by falling on his own sword.

Saul of the New Testament, whose name was changed to Paul, made peace with God and became an ardent follower of the Lord Jesus Christ. He, too, experienced fears. No man can face an angry mob clamoring for his death, suffer the beating of the whipping post, weather the storm and shipwreck at sea, and finally martyrdom, without having a battle with fear. But in spite of these experiences Paul was able to say, "I can do all things through Christ that strengtheneth me" (Philippians 4:13). His starting point was right relationship with God. Each of the two Sauls made his own choice as to which path he would follow. Both experienced fears; but what a difference in the outcome!

Too many times in dealing with fear we fail to go deep enough. Often the real problem is that a man's life is wrong. He has given way to evil; he is going in the wrong direction. His fellowship with God is broken. He must face the fact that he needs God's forgiveness because the Scripture says, "He that covereth his transgressions shall not prosper; but whoso confesseth and forsaketh them shall obtain mercy" (Proverbs 28:13).

"If we confess our sins, he is faithful and righteous to forgive us our sins, and to cleanse us from all unrighteousness" (I John 1:9).

Forgiveness comes through repentance. Repentance brings a change in the inner man, and this in turn affects both the conduct and character of man. "For as a man thinketh within himself, so is he" (Proverbs 23:7). Right thinking drives fear away when the right thinking comes as a result of inner change. The first step in overcoming fear is to *be sure* that you are right with God.

2. TAKE TIME ... *to develop a companionship*

No man needs to go through life alone. In fact, life is too much for any man to try it by himself. It is not enough to be right with God — one must learn to maintain a daily fellowship with Him.

The Psalmist tells us that this companionship is not given to the one who walks in the counsel of the ungodly, or the one who sits in the seat of the scoffer, but it comes to the one whose delight is in the law of Jehovah. To meditate daily in God's Word is to be like a tree planted by the waters. One's roots go down to the neverfailing supply. Jeremiah gives us a beautiful promise: "Blessed is the man that trusteth in Jehovah, and whose trust Jehovah is. For he shall be as a tree planted by the waters, that spreadeth out its roots by the river, and shall not fear when heat cometh, but its leaf shall be green; and shall not be careful in the year of drought, neither shall cease from yielding fruit" (Jeremiah 17:7-8).

It does not say that drought will never come nor that a hot, burning wind will never blow. It does say that we shall not fear nor be anxious when these things take place. The roots have tapped a certain supply of water, and these deep roots have produced fruit in spite of circumstances.

Our lives deepen with God as we learn to meditate and spend time in prayer. This produces faith — faith in God and His Word as well as in His faithfulness — and faith is the antidote for fear. Faith cancels out fear.

> Fear not, stand still, and see the salvation of Jehovah, which he will work for you today (Exodus 14:13).
>
> The fear of man bringeth a snare; but whoso putteth his trust in Jehovah shall be safe (Proverbs 29:25).
>
> Say to them that are of a fearful heart, be strong, fear not (Isaiah 35:3).
>
> Jehovah is my light and my salvation; whom shall I fear? Jehovah is the strength of my life; of whom shall I be afraid? (Psalm 27:1).

The curse of our time is busyness, and this usually causes shallowness. "Take time to be holy," is still good, sound advice. It is said that Enoch walked with God. How long has it been since you took a walk with God? Probably many of you can't even remember when you just took a walk. It is recorded that Adam and Eve "heard the voice of Jehovah God walking in the garden in the cool of the day" (Genesis 3:8).

Jesus was *walking* by the sea of Galilee when he saw two brothers. Throughout the Scriptures we find many references to walking, and though times have changed, there is still much therapeutic value in taking a leisurely stroll. I have found personally that a daily walk, taking time to meditate, to listen to the sounds about me and look at what God is doing in the nature world, helps much in maintaining balance both physically and spiritually.

Whatever you do, guard your quiet time. Don't always associate life with activity. Douglas Horton said, "We are like an old shoe — all worn out but the tongue." We desperately need silence and solitude because it is here that life is transformed. "Be still fidence shall be your strength" (Isaiah 30:15).

We overcome our fears by being right with God and developing a companionship with Him.

3. *PRACTICE GOOD WILL . . . let God's love flow through you*

"Now abideth faith, hope, love, these three: and the greatest of these is love" (I Corinthians 13:13).

Without a doubt, the greatest force in this world is love! How encouraging than to read that "God gave us not a spirit of fearfulness; but of power and love and discipline" (II Timothy 1:7). It is this love of God flowing through us that drives away fear and makes us whole. John, the disciple of love, wrote:

> There is no fear in love: but perfect love casteth out fear, because fear hath punishment; and he that feareth is not made perfect in love. We love because he first loved us (I John 4:18-19).

Who is afraid? Is it not the man who does not love? When God's love fills our hearts, there is no room for sin, doubt or fear. When we learn to love, we are armed against the enemies of hostility, resentment, anger, jealousy and fear.

If love casts our fear, then how do we learn to love? Jesus taught us the rules of love.

> Thou shalt love the Lord thy God with all thy heart, and with all thy soul, and with all thy mind, and with all thy strength . . . Thou shalt love thy neighbor as thyself. There is none other commandment greater than these (Mark 12:30-31).

Thou shalt love the Lord thy God with all thy heart, and with all thy soul, and with all thy strength, and with all thy mind; and thy neighbor as thyself . . . this do, and thou shalt live (Luke 10:27-28).

A new commandment I give unto you, that ye love one another; even as I have loved you, that ye also love one another (John 13:34).

This is my commandment, that ye love one another, even as I have loved you (John 15:12).

Jesus said, "If a man love me, he will keep my word" (John 14:23). Paul told the Galatians (5:14), "The whole law is fulfilled in one word, even in this: Thou shalt love thy neighbor as thyself." He continues to tell them that "the works of the flesh are manifest, which are these: fornication, uncleanness, lasciviousness, idolatry, sorcery, enmities, strife, jealousies, wraths, factions, divisions, parties, envyings, drunkenness, revellings, and such like . . . But the fruit of the Spirit is love, joy, peace, longsuffering, kindness, goodness, faithfulness, meakness, self-control."

When we allow the love of God to grow as a fruit within our lives, we enjoy the outgrowth of that love which is joy, peace, longsuffering, et cetera.

This word "love" in the Greek is *agape*. While difficult to translate into English, it teaches that at all times we are to adopt toward men unbreakable good will. We will love our neighbor as much as we love ourselves, and we will love ourselves as much as we love our neighbor. The same will be true of our enemies. Notice that John reminds us, "If a man say, I love God, and hateth his brother, he is a liar" (I John 4:20). When God flows through us, we will love even the unlovable, be it ourselves, our neighbors, or our enemies. This Divine love, which saw in me something worth saving, will also turn fear out the door and dispel every trace of terror.

In his book, *The Greatest Thing in the World,* Henry Drummond says:

Paul, in three verses, gives us an amazing analysis of what this supreme thing is . . . In these few words we have what one might call the Spectrum of Love. Observe its elements . . . notice that they have common names; that they are virtues which we hear about every day; that they are things which can be practiced by every man in every place in life; and how, by a multitude of small things and ordinary virtues, the supreme thing is made up.
The Spectrum of Love has nine ingredients:

Patience ...."Love suffereth long."
Kindness ...."And is kind."
Generosity ...."Love envieth not."
Humility ...."Love vaunteth not itself, is not puffed up."
Courtesy ...."Doth not behave itself unseemly."
Unselfishness ...."Seeketh not her own."
Good Temper ...."Is not easily provoked."
Guilelessness ...."Thinketh no evil."
Sincerity ...."Rejoiceth not in iniquity, but rejoiceth in the truth."

You will observe that all are in relation to men, in relation to life, in relation to the known today and the near tomorrow and not to the unknown eternity.

It is no wonder that God's love, flowing through us, helps us to develop a spirit of good will toward ourselves and toward mankind.

Someone has said, "You must love in order to understand love, and one act of charity will teach us more of the love of God than a thousand sermons."

Start today to love and you will not be afraid.

4. *TURN THE LIGHT ON . . . and examine your fears*

If fear is lack of confidence in the outcome of life's task and a sense of inadequacy for daily living, then we need to pinpoint and isolate, if possible, our fears.

One of the most dramatic personalities of history, Elijah the prophet, prayed, "It is enough; now, O Jehovah, take away my life" (I Kings 19:4). Remember, this man carried heaven's keys around and locked them up for a period of three years; and he had just wrought a mighty victory on Mount Carmel. Fire fell from heaven in answer to his prayer of faith, proving that Jehovah, and not Baal, was the true God. Weary from this victory (the cost of victory can sometimes make one weary, as well as defeat), he learned that Jezebel, the wife of King Ahab, was seeking to take his life. The man of God ran seventeen miles and finally, exhausted, he stopped under a juniper tree and asked that he might be allowed to die. If only he had asked himself, as the Psalmist did, "Soul, why art thou cast down?" the answer could have been his.

He really didn't want to die. If he had, he could have stayed around Carmel and Jezebel would have seen to his death. Fear and discouragement came as a result of weariness. God rested Elijah in a gentle sleep, and afterward spoke to him words of assurance in a still small voice.

Weariness causes a loss of nerve vitality, and if we are not careful we become apprehensive and fearful as a result. When we become too tired, we begin to think of ourselves and our feelings, and this is followed by despondency, at times even headaches, and depression. We then look at the symptoms and become more fearful, and a vicious circle begins.

We must come to terms with the cause of our fear and not continue to look at the symptoms. We cannot deal with the cause successfully while fear is present. Fear must be removed by first turning on the light and bringing the fear out into the open. Things always look bigger in the shadows.

Sometimes financial reverses set off a chain reaction of fear. You would be surprised how many times in our private counseling we trace the origin of fear to financial difficulties. Some get the feeling that God is against them and has decreed that they should fail. Maybe they have failed on an occasion, but now they are calling themselves a failure. To have failed does not mean one is a failure. I remember telling one man that I did not believe his problems occurred because he was born under an unlucky star, and he answered, "Pastor, there wasn't even a star out the night I was born."

Many of our fears would disappear if we would realize that the problem isn't God's judgment but our own bad judgment in overspending. I read that one devoted saint went window shopping on Fifth Avenue in New York. Returning to his hotel, he knelt to pray, "Lord, I thank You that I saw so many things I do not want."

Some could overcome fear by living more simply. One wife, reproved by her husband for her extravagance, replied, "It's the neighbor's fault — they're always buying things we can't afford!"

Some of us are masters at building mountains of fear out of grains of circumstances. Conversely, if we will allow God to work through us, we can build mountains of faith with only grains of trust. How do we do this? Well, I answer this by asking how you manage to build great mountains of fear with only grains of circumstances. First, we allow fear to enter our minds, to gain our attention. Second, we meditate on our fears, brooding over them and allowing them to increase. Third, when we have brooded sufficiently until they have become mountains of fear, we enclose them with walls of "What if?"

So, if we are to build mountains of faith, we can follow the same pattern. First, we must allow faith to enter our minds. The writer of Romans reminds us that "God hath given to every man a measure of faith." We already have faith, but we must put it to work. To strengthen our faith we must pray and read God's Word. Third, we should meditate on the power of God to meet our needs. Picture in your mind the ways that God could meet your needs. Expectantly wait for His answer. Begin to thank Him for the answer He has already prepared for you.

Then, enclose your mountain of faith with a wall of "But God . . ." When the enemy tries to make you fear and doubt, reply with a promise of God — "But God hath said . . ."

Fear and faith cannot dwell in the same spirit. When fear enters, faith leaves. In reverse, when faith enters, fear must flee. Jesus said, "If ye have faith as a grain of mustard seed, ye shall say unto this mountain, Remove hence to yonder place; and it shall remove; and nothing shall be impossible unto you" (Matthew 17:20). You can remove the mountain of fear in your life today by allowing God's Word to replace it with a mountain of faith.

> I sought Jehovah, and he answered me, and delivered me from all my fears (Psalm 34:4).
>
> Peace I leave with you; my peace I give unto you: not as the world giveth, give I unto you. Let not your heart be troubled, neither let it be fearful (John 14:27).

5. LOOK UP AND TRUST! . . . increase your expectancy

I had an appointment one morning with a lady who had been to see me several times. She was a lovely child of God but was suffering from deep-seated fears that dated back to her childhood. During previous visits we had discussed the problem of guilt and fellowship with God and loving her fellow man. She had promised to spend more time alone with God and to allow Him to do a work in her life. She assured me this had been done, but she was no better; in fact, if anything she was more fearful than ever. After confessing, praying and loving, she was still afraid. Fear begat fear, and she could not understand why God did not help her.

When I reviewed my schedule for the day and noticed that this lady was to see me, I knelt and asked God to empower me to help her. I looked over the notes taken from previous visits and claimed the promise of Jesus, "If any of you lack wisdom, let him ask of God, who giveth to all men liberally . . ." The answer came — I could hardly wait until she arrived.

She assured me again that she loved God, had spent time in prayer, and as far as she knew had no animosity toward anyone. But she was still very much afraid. The proof of her fear could be seen in her restlessness, fatigue, and at times her irritability. She was becoming more shy and was unable to digest food properly. She was frequently depressed.

Then I asked her: "When do you expect God to answer your prayer?" She wasn't sure. "Have you been praising God for the answer that is on the way?" I asked.

"No, because I don't feel that there is an answer on the way." Then we read Mark 11:23-24:

> Verily I say unto you, Whosoever shall say unto this mountain, Be thou taken up and cast into the sea; and shall not doubt in his heart, but shall believe that what he saith cometh to pass; he shall have it. Therefore I say unto you, All things whatsoever ye pray and ask for, believe that ye receive them, and ye shall have them.

I pointed out that the Lord told us clearly when we desired certain things we were to ask Him for these in prayer, and then we were to *expect* an answer. Now, if we really expect something to happen, we naturally will be thankful that it's coming. In other words, prayer, love, Bible reading in themselves are not sufficient. Expectation, faith, and hope are also part of the cure for fear.

I encouraged her to start that day expecting an answer, leaving the how and when to the heavenly Father. Then together we reviewed some of the great stories of both the Old and the New Testaments. There were times when others, like herself, didn't know which way to turn, or what to do. We talked, for instance, of Moses at the Red Sea, with the army of Pharaoh pursuing. Even though a few days prior God had shown Himself strong in their deliverance, the question was: What shall we do now? Moses talked it over with God, and the instructions were given: "Speak unto the children of Israel, that they go forward" (Exodus 14:15). They moved forward with expectation, knowing that the God who had delivered them before would not now fail.

We talked of young David, as he stood before the giant of Gath, Goliath, almost nine feet tall. David remembered that God had delivered him from the mouth of the lion and the paw of the bear, and that God was just the same. He chose five smooth stones and put his faith in God to direct those stones to do that which was needed.

Then I asked her: "Have you ever had an answer to prayer?" She began to share with me what God had done for her in her walk of faith. I could literally see expectation come to her heart.

We will not find the answer in prayer if we pray in fear, and continue to be fearful even after prayer. "All things whatsoever ye pray and ask for, believe that ye receive them, and ye shall have them" (Mark 11:24). Let us not forget that our Lord spoke those words. See also Psalm 62:5, "My soul, wait thou . . . for God only; for my expectation is from him."

Every great soul has experienced a bout with fear, but those who have overcome have done so through faith, love, and hope. "Why art thou cast down, O my soul? And why art thou disquieted within me? Hope thou in God; for I shall yet praise him for the help of his countenance" (Psalm 42:5).

Hope *in* God and praise *to* God bring good health, and it shows even on your countenance. "And now Lord, what wait I for? My hope is in thee" (Psalm 39:7).

> But I will hope continually, and will praise thee yet more and more (Psalm 71:14).

> By two immutable things, in which it is impossible for God to lie, we may have a strong encouragement, who have fled for refuge to lay hold of the hope set before us; Which we have steadfast (Hebrews 6:18-19).

Does God hear and answer every prayer? . . . Can prayer really change my life? . . . Why are my prayers not answered? . . . How can I be sure my prayer will be answered? . . . Is there a form of prayer we should follow? . . . To whom should I pray, the Father or Jesus Christ? . . . If God knows my need already, why should I pray? . . . How long and how often should we pray? . . . Are printed prayers answered? . . . How can I make my prayers more effective? . . . What kind of prayer pleases God most? . . . Should we pray about everything? . . . Does prayer really make a difference — or is it just good therapy? . . . Can prayer determine my destiny? . . . Can prayer change God's mind? . . . How can I keep my mind from wandering? . . . How long must I pray before God hears?

5 HOW CAN I PRAY EFFECTIVELY?

Charles Steinmetz, the great scientist, was once asked which field for future research offered the greatest promise. "Prayer," he replied instantly. "Find out about prayer!"

Prayer is a discovery. But like all discoveries, it is preceded by a search. Man must not only search his own soul and examine his attitudes and intentions, he must search God's holy Word for the type and manner of prayer which brings results. Discovering prayer is discovering the mightiest force in the universe.

Religion and prayer are generally closely associated. If a man is religious he feels he ought to pray, and usually a man who is successful in prayer is also successful in other areas of his life.

After observing the prayer life and the results manifested in the life of Christ, the disciples came to Him and said, "Master, teach us to pray." They did not ask to be taught to preach, to teach, to build an empire of wealth, or to be world famous. But they did ask how to pray.

Was something wrong with the way they were praying? They believed in prayer and had observed Christ as He prayed. They noted the value He placed on prayer and saw the effect prayer had on His life. They no doubt were listening when He said, "Father, I thank thee that thou heardest me. And I knew that thou hearest me always" (John 11:41-42).

They knew Jesus faced life with confidence. He was strong in the midst of severe pressures, with never a haggard or tired look upon his countenance. They wanted this inward strength, for they often found themselves weak, especially in times of temptation and stress.

How many times have we uttered the same cry: Oh, that I knew how to get through to God in prayer!

I remember one particular crisis when I knelt before God in prayer. I recall my frustration, realizing in that time of need that my mediocre life was inadequate. I simply had to find the Scriptural pattern for effective praying. I knew great men had unleashed the power of prayer and that this vital energy I so desperately needed was available to me as well. Deep within there was also an awareness that when this energy was missing there was no power, and where there is no power, there is an empty life. If I live a hundred years, I will not forget the change in my life that came during those days in a mountain cabin searching for the manner of prayer that brings results.

Prayer is everyone's privilege. We can all experience this force which unleashes the power of heaven on our behalf. As Alfred Lord Tennyson said, "More things are wrought by prayer than this world dreams of." But to experience the power of prayer we must learn to pray. This means prayer must not be pushed to a last resort. How much worry and how many tears would be eliminated if we would first learn to pray effectively.

Let me answer some of your questions on this important subject.

WHAT IS PRAYER?

Prayer is a personal appeal to a personal God. When you read the Bible you cannot help but notice that it is made up of stories of men and women who made personal appeals to a personal God and received personal answers. Prayer is asking God to help us when things are too big for us to handle. Prayer is placing in His hands our desires, which are not contrary to His will, with full assurance that He will answer because He loves us and desires the best for us.

Prayer is, first of all, a recognition of our needs. My prayer to God must be motivated by my sense of need. The greater my sensitivity toward that need, the greater will be the fervency of my prayer to God.

This principle applies regarding salvation. Before one can be saved he must recognize his need of salvation, and then direct his request to God through prayer.

A number of years ago, while elk hunting high in the mountains of Colorado, I lost my way in a blinding snowstorm. After hours of groping, I became confused and felt hopelessly lost. I remember that every sin of my past came before me in a panoramic view. I prayed. My prayer was born out of a sense of need. It was specific. It was personal. It was sincere. When I finally stumbled into a hunting camp of strange hunters (about three in the morning and nearly ten miles from my own camp) they asked,

"Who are you?" At that moment I was not interested in *who* I was but *where* I was. It is a terrible feeling to be lost.

The pathway to God is to admit that we are lost and ask Him to save us. When the prodigal son began to compare his lot in the pigpen with that of the servants in his father's household, immediately he reasoned: "How many hired servants of my father's have bread enough and to spare, and I perish with hunger! I will arise and go to my father . . ." (Luke 15:17-18). As soon as the prodigal son recognized his need, he had taken the first step toward home. As we come into God's presence, acknowledging that we have a need, we have taken the first step.

Prayer is to recognize that God is the true source of supply to meet our needs. When we pray we do not change God's mind. We do not need to say, "God, please change your mind and meet our needs." When we pray we do not change the purpose of God. You see, God has already purposed to do everything for His children that is good -- to save their souls, to bring them peace of heart, to heal their bodies, and to supply their every need.

As one writer said, "The eyes of Jehovah run to and fro throughout the whole earth, to show himself strong in the behalf of them whose heart is perfect toward him" (II Chronicles 16:9).

No, we do not change the purpose of God. He has already purposed to do good.

Having a sense of need, and recognizing that God is the source of supply, you are now ready to take the next step, for prayer also includes the *request* for God to meet your needs. Someone asked, "Pastor, since God already knows my needs, do I have to pray and ask Him for these things?"

Just as God has made irrevocable laws in the physical world, so He has made unchanging laws in the spiritual realm. Prayer consists of two parts — man's and God's. Man's part is to ask; God's part is to answer. The reason God does not answer before we ask is that He has made man a free moral agent. We have the power of choice, and God never invades without our invitation. He never forces Himself upon His children. Therefore, He waits our asking. When we have a need, we must come to God, who can meet that need, and ask for His help.

WHY SHOULD I PRAY?

I started to lay aside this question, thinking that everyone knows why prayer is important, but when I viewed the large number of questions, I sensed the genuine interest and concern in learning more about the importance of prayer. There are many reasons *why* we should pray. Let me list only a few.

To Live a Holy Life

If one's goal is to live a life pleasing to God, then he must learn to pray effectively. A holy life and prayer cannot be separated. One cannot survive without the other. Prayer is the greatest sin-killer in the world, and it is in prayer that we develop the right attitude toward ourselves, our work, and our world. It is in prayer that God searches us and brings to light the things in our lives which displease Him. David·found God to be the searcher, the revealer of his innermost thoughts.

> Search me, O God, and know my heart:
> Try me and know my thoughts;
> And see if there be any wicked way in me,
> And lead me in the way everlasting (Psalm 139:23-24).

Even our secret faults and our presumptuous sins are brought to the surface under the illuminating presence of God at prayer time. It is in times of prayer that we are "transformed into the same image from glory to glory, even as from the Lord" (II Corinthians 3:18).

To Prevent Spiritual Decline

We all know that declension is a forerunner of deterioration and that we are either progressive or retrogressive. When we cease to move forward, we begin to slip backward. We cannot stand still. Losing out spiritually generally is a gradual process. Behind every defeated Christian life is either prayerlessness or ineffective prayer.

Oftentimes our spiritual weakness results not only from what we do, but from what we fail to do. I shall never forget what Dr. Frank Laubach said in our pulpit — that when he ceases to pray, his personality is zero, and at that point there starts a retrogression. It is a vital prayer life that keeps this spiritual decline from taking place.

To Keep Ourselves Spiritually Energized

The Apostle Paul told the Corinthians in his second letter, "Though our outward man is decaying, yet our inward man is renewed day by day" (II Corinthians 4:16). To be spiritually on our tip-toes we need a continual refilling and refreshing. "Strive together with me in your prayers . . : that I may come unto you with joy, and may with you be refreshed" (Romans 15:30-32). The prophet of old said, "They that wait upon the Lord shall renew their strength" (Isaiah 40:31).

We often hear people say, "I am serving the Lord in my own weak way." God help us to quit serving in weakness, because every child of God can have power for service. This power comes through prayer. A man said to me, "I have no natural gifts." I answered, "Then pray that God will give you supernatural gifts that you may share in the victory for His cause."

How many times have we found it necessary to ask God for the wisdom that He has promised in the first chapter of James? Or to pray for special knowledge and understanding, or for Divine perception in matters that are beyond us? We often find ourselves needing God's immediate help in sudden emergencies. That is why the inner man must be renewed day by day. The only way I know to keep spiritually energized is to maintain an active life of prayer.

To Remain Spiritually Sensitive

Isn't it true that we become callous and our sensitivities are dulled without prayer? Neglect your prayer life for a few days and see what happens. Some things we would never do if sensitive to the will of God, we find ourselves justifying, excusing our behavior, because we have lost the sharpness of a sensitive heart.

The secret of the men of Bible times was that they knew which way God was going, and they went with Him. They kept in touch with Him. It was said of Enoch that he "walked with God" (Genesis 5:24). This requires keeping step with Him, neither lagging behind nor running ahead. It was said of Simon Peter that he "followed afar off" (Luke 22:54). True, he was going in the same direction, but not by any means keeping step with Christ. He slept while Christ prayed in the Garden of Gethsemane, and our Lord asked why he could not watch and pray during that critical time. Following afar off resulted in Peter's denying his Lord and allowing some of the old habits to take over momentarily. If we sleep when we should pray, we find it easier to follow afar off. If we continue this course, we lose our sensitivity to right or wrong. Prayer is vital if we are to remain spiritually sensitive to what God is doing or desires to do in our lives, in our work, and in the world about us.

Prayer equips us to carry on God's business. Jesus said, "I must work the works of Him that sent me while it is day: the night cometh, when no man can work" (John 9:4). He told us He could only do those things and say those things which the Father had given Him to do, and the writer of Acts reminds us that what Christ did, He did through the power and the ministry of the Holy Spirit (Acts 10:38). At the conclusion of Jesus' ministry He said, "As the Father hath sent me, even so send I you" (John 20:21). Just as Christ carried out His ministry for the Father in the power of the Holy Spirit, we, too, must wait in prayer until He anoints us for service.

If one has a desire to live a holy life, prevent spiritual decline, keep spiritually energized, and remain spiritually sensitive, then it is important to pray.

WHAT KIND OF PRAYER PLEASES GOD MOST?

Prayer in Jesus' Name

Jesus has taught us how to pray a God-pleasing prayer in John 16:23, "Whatsoever ye shall ask the Father in my name, he will give it you." The prayer that pleases God is the prayer that is prayed in Jesus' name. Our prayers are directed to the Father. "Our Father, who art in heaven, Hallowed be thy name" (Matthew 6:9). Although we address our requests to the Father, we always pray in Jesus' name because the name of Jesus means much to the Father. It is through His Son, Jesus, that our redemption was made complete and Satan's rule was broken. This is why we pray in Jesus' name. We remember those words of our Lord when He said in John 11:41, "Father, I thank thee that thou heardest me. And I know that thou hearest me always."

Prayer That Is Whole-hearted

God always desires prayer that is whole-hearted. The prophet Jeremiah said, "Ye shall seek me, and find me, when ye shall search for me with all your heart" (Jeremiah 29:13). When Jesus prayed in the Garden of Gethsemane, the Scripture says, "And being in an agony, he prayed more earnestly" (Luke 22:44). The Apostle James refers to "the effectual fervent prayer of a righteous man."

Jesus frowned upon the kind of praying that was mere words and repetitious phrases uttered without sincerity. He wants honesty of heart and soul — prayer born out of a sense of need with a realization that God is the source of supply.

There are so many sickly prayers these days — prayers that come only from the lips and have no soul in them. The word "agonize" was a common word to New Testament Christians but is not so common to us today. We are more familiar with the word "organize" than "agonize." Agonizing prayer is earnest and wholehearted. It is not just saying words from the lips.

That is not to say that to have heart and soul our prayers must be expressed with loud voice and strong emotion. There is nothing wrong with loud praying — it is possible that Jesus on occasions prayed this way — but we must never confuse heart and soul with volume. Hannah prayed earnestly but was only moving her lips. Her prayer was from her heart, not just from her lips. Many people pray the world over, but is it with their whole heart?

Prayer According to His Will

It pleases God when we accept His will as final. We have no grounds for answered prayer outside of God's will. There are some things about which we do not need to ask whether they are His will. We know it is His will to save us. His promise is: "Whosoever calleth upon the name of the Lord shall be saved."

"He chose us in him before the foundation of the world, that we should be holy and without blemish before him in love; having foreordained us unto adoption as sons through Jesus Christ unto himself, according to the good pleasure of his will" (Ephesians 1:3-5).

We know it is His will to supply our every need, providing we ask that need to be met for His glory. I am not surprised that many people do not receive answers to their prayers, for they pray selfishly. Some try to argue God into doing something which is not according to His Word. We must accept God's will as recorded in His Word. God is not going to tear up His moral laws just to satisfy the whims of one of His children. God has a law and abides by that law. "And this is the confidence that we have in him, that, if we ask anything according to his will, he heareth us: and if we know that he hear us whatsoever we ask, we know that we have the petitions that we desired of him" (I John 5:14-15).

Prayer in Faith

The prayer that pleases God is the prayer that is prayed in faith. God meets faith to the full extent of faith. "According to your faith be it unto you" (Matthew 9:29). The Word says, "But let him ask in faith, nothing doubteth: for he that doubteth is like the surge of the sea driven by the wind and tossed. For let not that man think that he shall receive anything of the Lord" (James 1:6-7).

Listen to these precious promises:

> And whatsoever ye shall ask in my name, that will I do, that the Father may be glorified in the Son. If ye shall ask anything in my name, I will do it (John 14:14-15).
>
> I have chosen you . . . that whatsoever ye shall ask of the Father in my name, he may give it you (John 15:16).
>
> Whatsoever ye shall ask the Father in my name, he will give it you (John 16:23).

These promises can be appropriated only on one condition — faith. They are given "to him that believeth."

The Bible does not teach that it is God's plan for men to be poor, sick, and full of failure. Neither does it teach that it is wrong to pray and believe for victory over these things. If we believe that we are to go through life half dead and ineffective, that is our privilege. But we cannot blame God! He has not only given us these gracious promises but has provided all things to all who believe.

I am not saying that God will not test us or that Satan will not buffet, but I am saying that God desires to supply our every need. If God had His way, it would be so. He waits only for our asking, and what good is there to ask if we do not believe.

Expect God to answer your prayer. Believe, not for just a little while, but without wavering, for "He is a rewarder of them that diligently seek Him" (Hebrews 11:6). Remember, we are not only to pray in faith, but it is sinful not to have faith when we pray. He has plainly stated that it is His will that we have spiritual and physical health, and that we be victorious. What He requires is for us to believe. We can understand, therefore, why it is wrong for us to doubt.

Prayer of Intercession

We all have at our disposal five ways of honoring God and blessing our fellowmen:

> By what we are, living epistles known and read of men;
> By what we say, the words we speak;
> By what we do, the service we render;
> By what we give, our money; and
> By intercessory prayer.

Follow the example of intercessory praying set by great men of the Bible. Abraham interceded for Sodom (Genesis 18:23). Ezra poured out his heart in intercession because of the sins of his people (Ezra 9). Nehemiah fasted and prayed for Jerusalem (Nehemiah 1:4). Daniel prayed for the captive Jews (Daniel 9:4). Paul interceded for Israel to be saved (Romans 10:1).

Christ was also an example in intercession. He prayed for sinners as prophesied by Isaiah (Isaiah 53:12); for weak believers (Luke 22:32); for His enemies (Luke 23:34); for all believers (John 17:9); and in heaven He still "intercedes" for all who come unto God by Him (Hebrews 7:25).

This is prayer at its highest, when we pray wholly for others. Jesus said, "The harvest indeed is plenteous, but the labourers are few. Pray ye therefore . . ." (Matthew 9:37-38). There are many people in this world who have no one to pray for them, no one to intercede before God in their behalf. May God give to each of us this blessed, unselfish ministry of intercessory prayer — the kind of prayer that brings joy to the heart of God.

WHY ARE PRAYERS NOT ANSWERED?

This question is asked more than any other, and perhaps I have already answered it. You see, prayer that pleases God is prayer according to God's will, prayed in faith. You may qualify in these two respects and yet fail because of other reasons. Perhaps your prayer is not answered because there is sin in your life. David said, "If I regard iniquity in my heart, the Lord will not hear me" (Psalm 66:18). If you have pushed some sin into the back yard of your life and think that you have covered it up and fooled God, may I remind you that you cannot make a fool of God? We cannot hide anything from His all-seeing eye. If we have unconfessed and unforsaken sin in our lives, we cannot expect to have God's approval.

> Behold, Jehovah's hand is not shortened that it cannot save; neither his ear heavy, that it cannot hear: but your iniquities have separated between you and your God, and your sins have hid his face from you, so that he will not hear (Isaiah 59:1-2).

Or maybe an unforgiving spirit hinders your prayer. Jesus said, "If thou bring thy gift to the altar, and there rememberest that thy brother hath ought against thee; leave there thy gift before the altar, and go thy way; first be reconciled to thy brother, and then come and offer thy gift" (Matthew 5:23-24). On another occasion He said, "And when ye stand praying, forgive, if ye have ought against any: that your Father also which is in heaven may forgive you your trespasses" (Mark 11:25).

God's forgiveness is dependent upon our forgiveness of our fellowmen. If we do not forgive them, we cannot be forgiven. Can we expect God to hear our prayers if we have an unforgiving spirit?

The Apostle Peter reminds us that it is necessary for husbands and wives not to be at odds with each other, for a bad spirit toward one another within the home hinders prayer. "Ye husbands, in like manner, dwell with your wives according to knowledge, giving honor to the woman . . . that your prayers be not hindered" (I Peter 3:7). A spirit of strife existing in the home between husband and wife will hinder receiving answers to prayer.

There is another reason why some people do not have their prayers answered. They are stingy! "Whoso stoppeth his ears at the cry of the poor, he also shall cry, but shall not be heard" (Proverbs 21:13). No man can keep everything he receives for himself, living only for his own pleasure, and expect God to hear his prayers. I have noticed that the people who pray are always people who give. You cannot pray and become like God without having a spirit of generosity. It's an impossibility! The nearest thing to the heart of God is a world that is lost. The proof of this is found in the truth, "God so loved the world that He gave . . . ." As we draw nigh to God, He deposits into our hearts compassion, concern, and love for the world about us and for His church. The automatic outgrowth of compassion, concern, and love is giving and sharing.

Does Prayer Really Work?

Someone asked, "Does prayer really make a difference, or is it just good therapy?"

The Apostle James wrote, "The effectual fervent prayer of a righteous man availeth much" (James 5:16). In the very next verse he says, "Elijah was a man subject to like passions as we are, and he prayed earnestly that it might not rain: and it rained not on the earth by the space of three years and six months. And he prayed again, and the heavens gave rain . . . ." Take special note of the phrase, "a man subject to like passions as we are." When I first read this I tried to argue with the Scripture. I said, "Elijah wasn't like me. After all, he prayed a half-minute prayer on one occasion and fire fell from heaven." But as I reviewed his life I realized that on another occasion he sat under a juniper tree and wished that he could die. You see, Elijah was, after all, a man like you and me. He had desires just as we have, common and ordinary.

But he was also a man who knew the power of prayer. Study Elijah's prayer life and you will find his secret. He recognized that he had a need, and he knew that God was the Source of supply for that need. He then prayed earnestly. He prayed that God would reveal Himself, which was God's will to do. He prayed in faith, and fire fell from heaven, honoring his faith.

If we pray to the Father in Jesus' name, in earnestness, according to God's will; if we pray in faith and maintain a proper attitude toward our fellowmen and a spirit of generosity — the Bible says that this kind of effective, fervent prayer will do all that needs to be done.

Prayer is the mightiest force in the universe. Why not put it to work in your own life? Follow Charles Steinmetz' suggestion: "Find out about prayer!"

Why does mental illness come to Christians? . . . Did Jesus say anything about mental illness? . . . What causes the mind to snap? . . . Does sin cause mental illness? . . . How should we deal with the emotionally or mentally ill? . . . Why are many Christians emotionally ill? . . . How can the inner man be strengthened? . . . Does the Bible discuss mental health? . . . I am about to lose my mind, can the Bible or God help me?

6 HOW CAN I DEAL WITH EMOTIONAL STRESSES?

As we read the Genesis account of creation one thing stands out. God created a perfect heaven and a perfect earth! There was no sin! There was no sorrow! There was no sickness; There was no death: "And God saw everything that he had made, and behold, it was good" (Genesis 1:31). We also read that God made man in His own image. As God is a trinity — God the Father, God the Son, and God the Holy Spirit — so God made man a trinity, a body, a mind, and a spirit. Just as God is sovereign with a will of His own, so God made man in His own likeness by giving him a will and a freedom of choice. This power of choice makes man sovereign within himself. No man can invade another man's will; nor, in the present scheme of things, does God Himself invade this human freedom. In this sense man was made in God's likeness.

Because man has freedom of choice and because God wanted man's worship to be voluntary, man had to be tested. He had to be given the opportunity of making a choice, either right or wrong. There were two voices in the Garden of Eden: God spoke and the serpent spoke.

Most of us know the story of how man yielded to the voice of the tempter, and how, when he did, something happened. Man fell from his lofty peak of fellowship with God into the valley of sin and remorse because of his disobedience to God. Sin then entered the world and brought with it death. Before that time there were no manifestations of death. Then the leaves withered and died; the flowers faded; the fruit decayed. Man, himself, became subject to death, as God said he would: "But of the tree of the knowledge of good and evil, thou shalt not eat of it: for in the day that thou eatest thereof thou shalt surely die" (Genesis 2:17).

Through the avenue of disobedience, sin entered this one-time peaceful, happy world. Not only was man's relationship to God changed, but his body and mind were also affected. As a result, man came to know sorrow of heart. Instead of tranquility of mind he began to experience frustration, distress, fatigue, restlessness,

69

edgy nerves, despair and melancholy. All of these negative, distressing emotions are the result of sin. The distress you experience today is not necessarily the direct result of your own sin, or even that of your parents; but every fear, every heartache, and all of the mind's frustrations date back to the day sin entered the world.

As the world "progresses" it becomes increasingly more complex. Today we live in a world of competitive economy. We are constantly trying to make ends meet, or else, to use a common expression, "to keep up with the Joneses." Because of this, we buy things we do not need, to influence people we do not like. This causes overwork and sometimes extra worry until things become so confused that we often take our problems to bed with us. Overworking, overeating (and too frequently overindulgence in other things, also), keep our nerves on edge.

We are a dissatisfied people for the most part. We want to be somewhere we aren't, to have somethings we can't have, and to make changes purely for the sake of change. Is it any wonder that today millions of people suffer from both physical and mental fatigue? I was not at all surprised that so many of the nearly five thousand votes cast in our recent sermon poll asked this question in one form or another: "Does Christianity offer help to the emotionally and mentally ill?"

There is no doubt that the high tempo of our modern-day living and the pressures of today's world have brought complications to our lives. Do you know that more than one-half of all hospital beds in America are occupied by emotionally and mentally ill people? That one out of every three families in America today will sometime in their lives commit one member of their family to a mental institution or engage professional help for a family member? America's number one health problem is mental illness, and over eighteen million Americans are being treated for it. Today there are approximately 600,000 patients in hospitals or institutions for emotional or mental reasons.

The question is: Can Christianity help? It is interesting to note that one psychiatrist said,

> Speaking as a student of psycho-therapy who has no concern with theology, I am convinced that the Christian religion is one of the most potent influences for producing that harmony, peace of mind and confidence of soul needed to bring health to a large proportion of nervous patients.

Before we can discover the cure for mental illness we must consider its causes. I have just finished reading the book, *Minds That Came Back*, by Dr. Walter C. Alvarez, a psychiatrist. Dr. Alvarez makes this statement: "Most emotionally induced illness does not come as the result of one large emotion. Far more often, it is the result of the monotonous drip, drip, drip of seemingly unimportant emotions — the everyday run of anxiety, fear, disappointments and longings. There is no set point where one suddenly enters into the land of mental or emotional illness. What is critical is the daily pattern of behaviour." It is this daily behaviour that I want to talk about.

I would not attempt to approach this subject from the viewpoint of a doctor or a psychiatrist, for I am neither. I approach the subject as a minister of the Gospel. I have gathered my conclusions from three areas: first, from a study of God's Word; second, from twenty years' experience of dealing and counseling with people; and third, from my own experience as a man who also faces the battle of life. From this background I have concluded that there are four major contributing factors to emotional and mental illness. God's Word deals with each of these contributing factors in a very thorough way, and provides a solution.

ANXIETY

The first is anxiety. In this one word can also be included worry and fear. I suppose all of us are aware of the fact that we have particular reactions to various emotions. Certain emotions, including fear, prepare us for action which sometimes saves our lives. It would be impossible for us to live successfully without a certain amount of anxiety and concern. I am anxious when I cross a busy street. I dare not dally because of the danger involved. We must recognize that these emotions are a part of our personalities. God has made us this way. But these emotions become wrong and harmful when they so grow out of proportion as to control our thinking, and thus the actions of our lives.

Constant worry and laboring under pressure is wrong and dangerous. All of us have experienced anxiety. We are acquainted with the physical reactions: our throats get dry; our heartbeats increase; we get knots in our stomachs; and our hands become clammy. Such momentary anxiety may be unpleasant, but it is not harmful. However, if we constantly live in a state of anxiety, if our nerves are tense and on edge from morning till night, our health is endangered.

The natural outgrowth of excessive anxiety is depression and physical exhaustion. Exhaustion leads to a feeling of inadequacy which easily develops into fear. Afraid that we do not have what it takes to meet life, we become moody, quarrelsome and self-conscious. We develop fear of other people and their opinions of us. We are concerned about being publicly humiliated. All of this is a result of living in a state of anxiety and being constantly filled with fear.

An editor who studied insanity in a mental hospital said that in the minds of most of the people with whom he chatted, the outstanding emotion had been fear — "an unreasoning, often vague, and formless fear."

What does Christianity have to offer to the man in this state of mind? What does the Bible say to him? The Bible speaks out clearly on the subject of anxiety and the Christian. "There is no fear in love; but perfect love casteth out fear: because fear hath torment" (I John 4:18). Who of us has not known the torment of fear? However, John reminds us that if we are filled with love there can be no fear, because love casts out fear.

When Jesus preached the great Sermon on the Mount, He very clearly said that we are not to live in a state of anxiety. "Don't worry and keep saying, 'what shall we eat, what shall we wear?' This is what pagans are always looking for; your heavenly Father knows that you need them all. Set your heart on His kingdom and His goodness, and all these things will come to you as a matter of course. Don't worry at all then about tomorrow" (Matthew 6:31-34, *Phillips Translation*). "And the peace of God, which passeth all understanding, shall keep your hearts and minds through Christ Jesus" (Philippians 4:7). As God's children we ought not to live in anxiety because we have a heavenly Father who has knowledge of our needs.

If I might reverse the coin, what Jesus was saying is that the only person who really ought to be anxious and worry is the person who does not have a heavenly Father. If you have a heavenly Father, then you can leave these things to His care. At the same time, one cannot cease being anxious by merely getting up some morning with the resolution, "I am not going to be anxious or worry any more." Jesus recognized that anxiety must be replaced with another emotion so he said, "Set your heart on His kingdom and His goodness . . . ."

We must redirect our thinking toward Jesus Christ and His kingdom. The things of God must have priority in our lives. As we center our lives in Christ, we begin to find a new way of life. We learn to put our trust in Him. Our lack of trust is actually the cause of our anxiety. When we look within for the answers to life's problems, when we trust in our own resources for our financial and physical needs, we sense that we are bankrupt, and our own inadequacies cause anxiety. On the other hand, if we are fully trusting in God for our needs, anxiety ceases because our trust is in an adequate source. For He is "able to do exceedingly abundantly above all that we ask or think" (Ephesians 3:20).

Our trust, then, is not in mere mental determination. Our dependence is upon God and His Word. As His children, "We know that to them that love God all things work together for good, even to them that are called according to his purpose" (Romans 8:28). Whether we have rain or sunshine, unemployment or employment, we are children of the King. Therefore we cease to be anxious! Our faith is in God, our heavenly Father. The same God, who notices when a sparrow falls to the ground and knows the exact number of hairs on our head, is interested in us.

Before Jesus went back to heaven He gave His disciples and all of us this wonderful assurance, "Lo, I am with you alway" (Matthew 28:20). We have the promise of His continuous presence with us. We are also told, "Let Him have all your worries and cares, for He is always thinking about you and watching everything that concerns you" (I Peter 5:7, *Living Letters*).

We do not overcome anxiety by positive thinking alone, but by positive faith. We overcome anxiety by removing the source of worry. We must "let Him have" — give unto His care — our needs and worries. We know the sense of well-being that comes when the bills are paid, when we recover from a serious illness, or when we know that a loved one is safe and secure. We can know this same relief when we learn to place our cares and worries in God's hands even before the answer comes.

No wonder Paul wrote to Timothy, "God hath not given us a spirit of fear; but of power, and of love, and of a sound mind" (II Timothy 1:7). How do we overcome anxiety? We replace the emotion of anxiety with trust, and practice putting the kingdom of God first, making Christ the center of our lives. As we do, we begin to know peace of mind and satisfaction of soul.

RESENTMENT

The second contributing factor is resentment. If allowed to fester, resentment turns into bitterness; and bitterness, if not stopped, turns into hatred. Doctors, as well as all of us, know from personal experience the effects of anger and resentment. Our nervous systems become sensitive; our hearts beat a little faster; our digestion slows down; we get keyed up and ready to fight. This is why the Bible warns us, "lest any root of bitterness springing up trouble you" (Hebrews 12:15). This is so serious to God that we are admonished to beware of even a little root getting established.

The race riots in the United States are nothing more than an outgrowth of bitterness. We will never solve our problems of resentment by legislation. It requires a change of heart! We must stop hating!

A man who works in a service station where I sometimes buy gas told me, "I was in the Japanese war in the South Pacific. I was taught to hate the Japanese. My brother was in another conflict and was taught to hate the Germans. Now, neither of us knows how to love — we have learned to hate."

Unfortunately, this is what is happening in our world. Men strive for emancipation and freedom, and when they don't get it, they resent those who have it. Then there is a clash. If we don't fight with our fists or guns, we fight with words. Sometimes we fight only with thoughts, and a civil war rages inside. All of this affects our mental health.

This is why the wise man Solomon said, "Better is a dinner of herbs, where love is, than a stalled ox and hatred therewith" (Proverbs 15:17). In other words, it is better to eat vegetables for dinner in an atmosphere of peace than to have filet mignon and strife. How many of our meals have been spoiled because those seated around the table possessed resentment toward one another!

In the Old Testament there is a command which we need to learn. "Thou shalt not hate thy brother in thy heart" (Leviticus 19:17). When Paul wrote to the church at Ephesus he said, "Let there be no more resentment, no more anger or temper, no more violent self-assertiveness, no more slander and no more malicious remarks. Be kind to each other; be understanding. Be as ready to forgive others as God for Christ's sake has forgiven you" (Ephesians 4:31-32 *Phillips Translation*).

Jesus dealt with the problem of resentment in the fifth chapter of Matthew. After saying that resentment is wrong, that we should not hate, Jesus commanded us to do the opposite: "Love your enemies, bless them that curse you, do good to them that hate you, and pray for them which despitefully use you and persecute you" (Matthew 5:44). This is somewhat of a paradox to most of us. A lady wrote me not long ago and said, "There is a person that I must love — I know I should, and I want to, but I resent this person and cannot seem to love him. How do we learn to love?" The answer is simple: we learn to love by loving.

When we love a person, the result is twofold: first, we forgive him; second, we become concerned about his welfare and feel a sense of responsibility toward him. Love must begin on our knees because it is through prayer that we forgive. We must repent of our feelings of resentment and pray that the love of God will flow through us to the other person. We soon discover that we cannot long pray for a person without changing our feelings toward him. When we pray, God allows us to feel the needs of that person, and we develop a desire to help him.

We then need to follow our prayers with action. If we are sincere, God will help us find ways to express love and concern for those we have formerly resented. God's love will melt our resentment and replace it with an attitude of kindness and love.

A lady crippled by arthritis drove from Cheyenne to my office one day for counseling. We talked about her problems, and out of it came her story of deep resentment toward her mother. Her mother was advanced in years, but the daughter's resentment dated back to childhood. I asked this lady to follow me in prayer. She did until we came to the name of her mother. I had asked God to help her love her mother, and prayed for her mother's welfare and happiness. She would not continue in prayer nor say a word. I started over and asked her to repeat my prayer. Again when I asked God to bless her mother she stopped. I just waited. It seemed an eternity before the silence was broken and she then burst into tears. After she regained her composure, I led her in prayer again, and when I prayed for her mother, she broke once more. Finally, she was able to pray for her mother's healing. She prayed that she would be cleansed from all resentment toward her mother. Later that day, when she arrived home, she called me and said, "Pastor, as I drove I continued to pray audibly for my mother as you suggested. Not only did the resentment leave, but the stiffness in my joints and neck began to leave. I have not only found help for the inside, but it has affected my body as well."

There are only two feelings that we can have toward others — we either love them or resent them. Someone is sure to answer, "Well, Preacher, I don't hate them — I am just not interested in them." No, there is no neutrality here.

Why not practice the presence of God? Allow God's love and grace to flow through you to others. When you do, you will know peace of mind and happiness. The distress which resentment causes will be gone.

An Inferiority Complex

This brings me to the third contributing factor to mental illness — an inferiority complex. Feelings of inferiority are quite prominent in many people with whom I have talked. Because life moves so fast and we are here only a short while, I am convinced that we ought to be living full, happy lives. Yet, multitudes of men and women cannot live full, happy lives because they are emotionally upset and hindered by feelings of inferiority.

The feeling of being inferior is often a sign of being self-centered, proud, and filled with self-love. When pride is hurt we have a tendency to become seclusive, self-conscious, sensitive to criticism, and to make unfavorable comparison with others. With hurt feelings a critical spirit develops, and we try to dominate and govern others or withdraw and avoid others because of the fear of failure.

Now we all feel inferior at times. We not only *feel* inferior — we *are* inferior to someone in some area. When Jimmie McDonald, our staff soloist, begins to sing, I feel inferior. I cannot sing as he can. I cannot play the piano like Robert Cunningham, our church pianist; nor can I play golf as well as my assistants on the pastoral staff. But should I stay in bed and say, "There is no use in getting up," because I lack these abilities?

Fortunately, God did not make any of us exactly like any other. You are you, and I am I. Hollywood may say that we must measure up to a particular standard to be handsome or beautiful; the business world may suggest that we must make a certain sum of money to be successful; but God does not use that set of standards.

It is interesting to note, as we read the New Testament, that no details are given of Christ's physical appearance. I suppose if the Bible had said that Jesus was exactly six feet tall, men would be trying either to grow taller or to shrink until they, too, were that height. We do not know the physical height of our Lord, or the color of His eyes, or the measure of His chest. Instead, the New Testament gives us a spiritual standard with which to measure our lives. "The Lord seeth not as man seeth; for man looketh on the outward appearance, but the Lord looketh on the heart" (I Samuel 16:7). God is interested in the condition and growth of our inner selves. God has given to each of us certain abilities, and certain tasks to perform. He does not ask me to perform my neighbor's task with my abilities, nor does He expect me to apologize because I cannot.

We all share to some degree this feeling of inferiority. The question is: how do we conquer it? How do we keep it from hindering our progress and causing mental distress? To answer this we must consider what happens when we are controlled by the love of God.

First, we love God. Second, we love our neighbors; and third, we love ourselves. When I told one man this he replied, "But, Pastor, if I think too much about myself, if I start believing in myself like you are trying to tell me, then I am going to be proud, and God will strike me down." He then quoted Proverbs 16:18, "Pride goeth before destruction, and a haughty spirit before a fall."

"Either way," he said, "I am going to fail."

This man erred in not making a distinction between the two kinds of pride. There is a pride that goes before a fall. This is the superiority attitude. It is demonstrated when we say, in effect, "Glory be to me. I am what I am because of me! My talents, my ability, everything I have is because of me!" This is the kind of pride that God strikes down. When we recognize that it is God who permits us to become wealthy, that it is God who has given us the talents and abilities we possess, and that every good and perfect gift comes down from the Father above, then God is pleased. I must realize that I have but one life to give for Him, and I must make it count. When I have the right attitude toward myself, my inferiority feelings vanish and I can do my best for the Master.

"I am what I am by the grace of God!" This brings peace to my mind and puts my feet on solid ground. Remember, *your* best may not be *the* best. But if it is *your* best, that is all God requires. If you have only one talent, then God will not require you to give a five-talent performance. We must not always compare ourselves with others, but maintain a right attitude toward ourselves, toward our work, and toward the world around us. This will keep us in balance, giving a healthy outlook both mentally and spiritually.

"When pride cometh, then cometh shame" (Proverbs 11:2).

"Whosoever shalt exalt himself shall be humbled; and whosoever shall humble himself shall be exalted" (Matthew 23:12).

"A high look, and a proud heart, even the lamp of the wicked is sin" (Proverbs 21:4).

"God resisteth the proud, but giveth grace to the humble" (James 4:6).

Humility rules out hidden inferiority feelings because a humble man does not suffer from hurt pride, and his feelings are not easily ruffled. We come to Jesus and find rest for our souls and peace for our minds.

It is always refreshing when we meet someone with a healthy attitude toward himself. A sixth grade teacher asked her class if they could think of something lovely in the world that was not here twenty years ago. One little boy raised his hand and said, "Yes — me."

A cure for an inferiority complex is a right attitude toward myself, toward my work, and toward my world.

GUILT

The fourth contributing factor to mental illness is guilt — that gnawing feeling deep within which reminds us that we are not quite square with ourselves or the world.

Sir Arthur Conan Doyle tells of a practical joke he played on his friends. The story goes that he sent a telegram to twelve famous people, all of whom were men of great virtue and reputation and of considerable position in society. The message was worded: "Fly at once, all is discovered!" Within 24 hours all twelve of the so-called virtuous men had left the country! Guilty conscience? Evidently.

How many people have come to me and said, "My nerves are on edge; I am sick mentally and physically." After I have counseled with them for awhile, the truth often comes out — they are battling guilt. They are carrying a burden of guilt which keeps them mentally distressed, and eventually affects their physical health.

We all have our pet ways of trying to absolve guilt. Some husbands, to cover up a breakfast quarrel, come home from work with a box of candy or a dozen roses. This, of course, is easier than saying, "I am sorry; please forgive me." A businessman, in order to sooth his conscience about a shady transaction, may give a large donation to his church. Others go to a confession booth or simply tell it to a friend in order to get it off their chests. No one really enjoys guilt. It is uncomfortable and destructive.

There is only one lasting solution to the problem of guilt, and that is the Biblical solution. Guilt usually falls into one of three categories, and for each of these the Bible has an answer.

First, we suffer guilt for actual sins committed. This is true of us all! "For all have sinned and fall short of the glory of God" (Romans 3:23). When we measure ourselves by God's standard, we feel guilty and ashamed in His presence. We are uncomfortable in church. Isaiah says, "Come now and let us reason together, saith the Lord: though your sins be as scarlet, they shall be as white as snow; though they be red like crimson, they shall be as wool" (Isaiah 1:18). The Apostle John reminds us, "If we confess our sins, he is faithful and just to forgive us our sins, and to cleanse us from all unrighteousness" (I John 1:9). The only solution to the problem of transgression is forgiveness. With God, forgiveness is complete; we need never be troubled by guilt again. "As far as the east is from the west, so far hath he removed our transgressions from us" (Psalm 102:13).

The second type of guilt is condemnation. We may feel guilty because of actual sin or because we have failed to appropriate God's forgiveness. It is the enemy's business to try to bind us with guilt.

We must beware of continual fretting and brooding over past sins. If we have confessed and have asked forgiveness, let us not continue to condemn ourselves. To do so indicates a lack of faith. Be as gracious with yourself as God is with you. Paul said, "Being therefore justified by faith, we have peace with God through our

Lord Jesus Christ . . . . There is therefore now no condemnation to them that are in Christ Jesus . . . who walk not after the flesh but after the Spirit" (Romans 8:1, 4).

The third source of guilt is closely related to the second — regret and sorrow. Many people browbeat themselves. They are broken and unable to function properly, sad of countenance and heart because of their past. It is true that we have all made mistakes in the past, but when we have found forgiveness, we need also to forget. The Apostle Paul is our example. Admitting that he had made mistakes, he said, "One thing I do, forgetting the things which are behind, and stretching forward to the things which are before, I press on toward the goal unto the prize of the high calling of God in Christ Jesus" (Philippians 3:13-14). We must do with our past what God has done: forget it. God is not interested in that which has been forgiven; He is interested in our future.

There is, then, one solution for guilt; that is the blood of Jesus Christ. We can be forgiven if we will confess our sins and believe on Him. He alone has the ability to obliterate sin, to remember it against us no more. He can perform spiritual surgery and cleanse us from all sin, removing guilt forever.

However, forgiveness of sin involves more than God's willingness to forgive us. It also involves our willingness to accept God's forgiveness and to forget the past. When guilt becomes self-pity and we brood over it, this itself becomes sin. God expects us to accept His forgiveness, pick up the pieces of our lives, and allow Him to mend them, developing in us a new life in Him.

We do not need to fear mental or emotional illness if we will obey the principles God has given us in His Word. For each of the contributing factors God has provided a cure. For anxiety, there is God's sufficiency. He is willing to carry our load and is personally interested in the details of our lives. If resentment troubles us, we need only ask and God will give us His love, flowing through us in healing power. If an inferiority complex overcomes us, He "renews a right spirit within us," restoring the self-confidence He has ordained for us. For guilt and burdens that distress, God offers complete forgiveness. He makes the record clean and gives us a new start in life.

Jesus said, "I came that they might have life, and have it abundantly." God wants us to be happy, to enjoy peace of mind and health. "Beloved, I pray that in all things thou mayest prosper and be in health, even as thy soul prospereth" (III John 2). Yes, the Bible has the answer to mental illness: there is an abundant life in God.

PRACTICE USING THIS FORMULA:

1. *Remove the guilt complex* . . . by confessing your sins to God, through Jesus Christ. His righteousness becomes imputedly yours by faith. This makes God your heavenly Father and establishes a fellowship and union with Him.

2. *Walk with Him in fellowship* . . . it is a humbling process and removes the feeling of being inferior.

3. *Allow His love and presence to drive out resentment and bitterness toward others* . . . giving you a love for all men — even your enemies.

4. *Seek to do His will and please Him* . . . "Seeking first His kingdom," knowing "that all things work together for good to them that love God," brings to us a knowledge that He cares for us and has promised never to leave us. Therefore, we will not be anxious or worry. This in return brings to us a peace of mind beyond understanding, rest for the soul, and the fulfillment of the promise: "God hath not given to us a spirit of fear but of a sound mind."

Just what is faith? . . . How does faith work? . . . Does your personality affect your faith? . . . How can we develop a strong faith? . . . Do our degrees of faith change? . . . Does faith really move mountains? . . . How can I increase my faith? . . . How much faith is necessary? . . . If faith is the gift of God, what part do we play? . . . Can we do anything to increase our faith? — or must God do it all? . . . Is faith in God just optimism? . . . Does our faith really make a difference in God's actions? . . . How important is faith? . . . How does God evaluate our faith? . . . Can everyone have faith? . . . What if you just don't have any faith?

7 HOW DO I HAVE FAITH?

An interesting story in the Old Testament unfolds around a burdened prophet by the name of Habakkuk. This man of God became disturbed about what seemed to be God's inactivity in the affairs of men. All around him the prophet saw a continual increase in violence and iniquity. There was strife and contention, lawlessness and injustice everywhere. It seemed to him that the wicked continued to prosper and that God was little concerned about it all.

Furthermore, the wicked were continually devouring the righteous while God, from the prophet's viewpoint, remained aloof and silent. As a result he began to question God and even became argumentative in his spirit. Listen to his prayer:

> O Jehovah, how long shall I cry, and thou wilt not hear? I cry out unto thee of violence, and thou wilt not save. Why dost thou show me iniquity? Destruction and violence are before me; and there is strife, and contention. Therefore the law is slacked, and justice doth never go forth; for the wicked doth compass about the righteous; therefore justice goeth forth perverted (Habakkuk 1:2-4).

In verse 6 of the same chapter God told the prophet that judgment would come to the wicked and that He would use those bitter and impetuous people, the Chaldeans, to bring about this judgment. As for God's own people, there was a divine plan in the making. A vision was to become a reality at God's appointed time. The Lord Himself would reward His own, and the prophet was told to wait, for although the vision would tarry, it would in due time become a reality (Habakkuk 2:3).

This vision pointed to the return of our Lord. The writer of Hebrews, quoting the prophecy of Habakkuk, changed the word *it* to the word *He*, leaving no doubt as to the meaning of the Scripture. The Lord would return and reward His own for their faithfulness.

This caused the concerned seer to ask one more question: How can we (and our children) live until the Lord returns?

The answer was given in simple language. "The righteous shall live by his faith" (Habakkuk 2:4).

What a difference this made in his outlook. He still saw the injustice and violence of his time, but he saw it in the light of God's plan. This completely changed his attitude. Listen as he concludes by saying:

> For though the fig-tree shall not flourish,
> Neither shall fruit be in the vines;
> The labor of the olive shall fail;
> And the fields shall yield no food;
> The flock shall be cut off from the fold,
> And there shall be no herd in the stalls:
> Yet I will rejoice in Jehovah,
> I will joy in the God of my salvation.
> Jehovah, the Lord, is my strength;
> And he maketh my feet like hinds' feet,
> And will make me to walk upon my high places
>
> (Habakkuk 3:17-19).

What a change in outlook! Faith in God made the difference. Faith made sense. This affected his attitude and, therefore, his outlook changed. He now understood that the hope of Israel would be realized in the fulfillment of God's plan.

Even though science has given us a different world in which to live, we still live by faith. In fact, it is impossible to live without faith, not only in the spiritual realm, but also in the social and the personal realm of our everyday life. We mail a letter and believe it will arrive at its destination. We press the elevator button and have faith that we will arrive safely. We drink from the public water fountain without demanding an analysis. We deposit our savings in a bank, believing in the promise of safe-keeping. We purchase tickets for an airline flight, and even though we do not know the pilot or co-pilot, we have faith that we shall alight safely at our destination.

You see, if we were to strike from mankind the principle of faith we would have no more history than a flock of sheep. That which holds human society together is faith, and nothing is more basic or indispensable if there is to be corporate human life at all. That brings us to our first question —

WHAT IS FAITH?

The word *faith* occurs in one form or another 749 times from Genesis to Revelation. It means "to confide in; to take one at his word; to trust another to the extent that we are secure from fear; to put absolute trust in a person without questioning."

The only definition found in the Scripture is recorded in Hebrews 11:1. "Now faith is assurance of things hoped for, a conviction of things not seen." The *Living Letters* translation reads: "What is faith? It is the confident assurance that something we want is going to happen. It is the certainty that what we hope for is waiting for us, even though we cannot see it up ahead."

Faith, then, simply means taking God at His Word and acting upon it. One of our radio listeners sent me one of the best definitions I have seen: "Faith is a willingness to trust God when questions cannot be answered by the knowledge that is available to us." Another I especially like: "Faith is a quality by which the things desired become things possessed."

Another radio listener penned these lines:

> *Faith* is more than just a word,
> It is a feeling, deep and true
> That with every passing hour
> Hope is born anew.
>
> Faith means having courage
> To know, as days go by —
> That just as long as *faith* lives on,
> Then *hope* can never die.

How Does Faith Work?

More people were concerned about how faith works than having faith defined. In other words: what are the mechanics of faith? Do we pray to God and then relax, expecting God to work things out in His own time and way?

On some occasions faith works exactly that way. By faith the matter is turned over to God, and man has nothing more to do with the situation. The Bible is full of illustrations of how God miraculously honored the prayer and faith of His children.

However, God does not work that way on every occasion. Frequently prayer and faith must be followed by a third component — action. "Faith, if it have not works, is dead in itself" (James 2:17). The Bible informs us that there were many who believed who also had tasks to perform. In other words, they had a part to play in the answering of their prayers. Their names are recorded in the great faith chapter, Hebrews 11. These men not only prayed, expecting an answer, they also put their faith into action. To them faith was relying on God's promises and acting accordingly. Faith was taking a positive step.

In Hebrews 11:6 we read: "Without faith it is impossible to please God; for he that cometh to God must believe that he is, and that he is a rewarder of them that diligently seek him."

This verse is followed by an illustration. "By faith Noah, being warned of God concerning things not seen as yet, moved with godly fear, prepared an ark to the saving of his house; through which he condemned the world, and became heir of the righteousness which is according to faith." Faith to Noah was not expecting a miracle of deliverance to be dropped from the skies; faith was going into action and obeying God's Word.

One day God appeared to a man by the name of Abram and said, "Get thee out of thy country, and from thy kindred, and from thy father's house, unto a land that I will show thee: and I will make of thee a great nation, and I will bless thee, and make thy name great; and thou shalt be a blessing" (Genesis 12:1-2). Abram did not sit there in the tent and expect God to transport him to the promised land. He himself had a part to play. He had to pack his belongings, gather his family, say good-by to his relatives, and go. Abram left, not knowing where he was going, but taking the necessary steps of action, believing God would guide him the whole way.

A little lady with a terrible affliction learned one day that Jesus, the Healer, was in her community. She believed that if she could get to Him, He would heal her. When she arrived she discovered that He was surrounded by a multitude of people. She elbowed her way through the crowd, determined to get close to Jesus. She believed that if she could only touch the hem of His garment she would be healed! To her, faith meant touching. It meant action!

As you read through the Bible you will discover that over and over again faith involved action. It meant taking a step in obedience to God's Word. When that afflicted woman *did* touch the hem of Jesus' garment, she was immediately healed. Jesus turned and said to her, "Daughter, be of good cheer; thy faith hath made thee whole" (Matthew 9:22). Her faith made the difference, and in her case it was active faith. Pressing through the crowds and touching the hem of His garment were actions prompted by her faith.

Other times, faith means walking in obedience while God is

working things out. I went into a hospital room not long ago to visit a dear lady who was suffering from a kidney infection. When I arrived, she and her husband were talking things over. There was the possibility of a serious operation, depending upon the disclosures of a forthcoming report from the laboratory. When I inquired how things were, they replied, "We believe that the reports coming from the laboratory will be favorable." I could see that their faith was wrapped up in the laboratory report. I suggested that we read the Scriptures and pray. I prayed earnestly that their faith would be in God and the power of His Word, and not in what we could see or hear. In other words, the reports from the laboratory would not necessarily be final. God is greater than all. Our faith must be in Him, in His will, even when questions cannot be answered by the knowledge that is available to us.

When a man lets his faith sink deep into God's Word, he learns one of the great secrets of life. Many times people say to me, "Pastor, I am believing for thus and thus." And I answer by asking, "Upon what is your faith based? What Scriptures are you standing on?" Often they look rather puzzled, for they do not have a verse or a portion of God's Word on which to base their faith. They cannot say, "I am basing my faith on one or more of God's immutable promises!"

I am convinced that faith based upon the Word of God brings results. This kind of faith works. James said, "Show me thy faith apart from thy works, and I by my works will show thee my faith" (James 2:18). A passive faith may be nothing more than an opinion about God. Some people say, "Oh, yes, I believe in God," but their lives are no different. When you analyze their belief, you see that what they have is an opinion about God, and not Christian faith. Christian faith is more than an opinion; it is more than mental assent to truth.

You may pick up a college catalog and give mental assent to the contents of that catalog, yet never experience college life on that particular campus. Your mouth may water as you read the menu of a certain restaurant, but you may never eat there. In the same way you may agree with this or that creed of the Christian religion, and yet not experience Christianity because your faith is only mental assent. You have an opinion. Opinion is necessary, but opinions alone do not bring results. Yet it is impossible to have faith based on God's Word without results.

A positive Christian faith — a faith that works — is a faith in a personal God, confidence in His Word, in His power, in His grace, and a faith that moves into action.

Also, faith works best when it is definite. Effective faith is specific faith. Notice Hebrews 11:1 again: "Now faith is assurance of things hoped for, a conviction of things not seen." Let me ask a question: What things are you hoping for?

You must decide what you want in life and then determine if that desire is in harmony with God's Word. He has promised to give you the desires of your heart, but you must determine what those desires are. Jesus said, "All things whatsoever ye pray and ask for, believe that ye receive them, and ye shall have them" (Mark 11:24). Those desires, with God's approval, become the subject of my daily prayer and the focus of my faith. They become the "things I hope for," the things I pray for, the things I expect to receive. I am more than ready to give of myself to do anything God wants me to do to help bring them into reality. If a miracle is needed, then I shall believe for a miracle. "But let him ask in faith, nothing doubting. For he that doubteth is like the surge of the sea driven by the wind and tossed. For let not that man think he shall receive anything of the Lord" (James 1:6-7).

If your desires are clear and firm, and with a proper motive to please God, then believe and refuse to doubt. Do not decide on one way today and another way tomorrow — set your goals and believe. Nine out of ten people I interview have not established what they really want in life, and they remind me of this picture in James, "a sea driven by the wind." They are constantly changing and then wonder why there is but little progress in the development of their faith.

The sure formula of success according to the Scriptures is: God-honoring desire plus faith minus doubt equals success. Read that again:

$$\text{DESIRE} + \text{FAITH} - \text{DOUBT} = \text{SUCCESS}$$

Ponder over it. Write it on a card to carry with you or place on your mirror, and ask yourself again and again: Are my desires pleasing to the Lord? If so, am I really putting my faith in God, and have I removed my doubts? If you can say, Yes, the answer is on the way. That is the way faith works. It takes God at His Word and counts Him faithful. It expects the complete answer, even though it cannot be seen at once, because — and we must always remember this — the *when* and the *how* God reserves for Himself.

Do not doubt by looking at the symptoms, feelings, or the impossibilities. No, do not look even at the time element involved, for faith is the conviction that what God has promised is done already. Faith laughs at impossibilities. It leaves the way and means with God, realizing that those are *His* responsibilities, and our part is not to hinder Him by doubting and questioning.

Begin to rejoice because the answer is on the way. Be happy over it. See the answer by the eye of your soul, and praise God for hearing your prayers.

You cannot have faith without results, for faith always works.

How Can I Increase My Faith?

The Bible speaks of various kinds of faith — common faith, weak faith, temporary faith, active faith, wavering faith, unwavering faith and strong faith. Since faith works, it is only natural that we desire a strong, mountain-moving faith that gets results, that laughs at circumstances and refuses to be defeated.

On two occasions Jesus referred to "great faith," and in both instances it was because the individual had implicit, childlike faith in God and His Word. On one occasion a centurion came, seeking healing for his servant. He said, "Lord, I am not worthy that thou shouldest come under my roof; but only say the word, and my servant shall be healed" (Matthew 8:8). "And when Jesus heard it, He marvelled, and said to them that followed, Verily I say unto you, I have not found so great faith, no, not in Israel" (Matthew 8:10).

Jesus always rejoiced in faith. He knew the power of faith because it was the secret of His own soul. When He saw this Gentile filled with great faith He was thrilled.

Great faith is also illustrated in the life of Abraham, referred to by the Apostle Paul in Romans 4:18-22.

> Who in hope believed against hope, to the end that he might become a father of many nations, according to that which had been spoken, so shall thy seed be. And without being weakened in faith he considered his own body now as good as dead (he being about a hundred years old), and the deadness of Sarah's womb; yet, looking unto the promise of God, he wavered not through unbelief, but waxed strong through faith, giving glory to God, and being fully assured that what he had promised, he was able also to perform. Wherefore also it was reckoned unto him for righteousness.

Notice, he staggered not at the promises of God through unbelief, but was strong in faith. This supreme faith is possible to every child of God. The question is: How can I increase my faith until it is strong and active to the glory of God?

We are not told in the Scriptures to pray for faith, but to "have faith in God." Therefore, the Scriptures teach that the following steps will develop within us a strong faith.

1. *Know God*

Faith is not a definition, or a formula, or just a testimony of what others have experienced. Christian faith begins by accepting Christ as personal Saviour.

One becomes a Christian by faith, and when by faith he becomes God's child, he is a new creature. Our faith then is directed toward God and our Saviour, the Lord Jesus Christ. That is why we read, "And without faith it is impossible to be well pleasing unto him; for he that cometh to God must believe that he is, and that he is a rewarder of them that seek after him" (Hebrews 11:6).

We cannot know God unless we believe He exists, and we cannot receive answers to our prayers unless we believe He will reward us for our seeking. Seeking Him brings us into a right relationship with Him, and this becomes the foundation of our faith. It is through prayer and praise that we come to know Him. Therefore, we do not pray for faith, but we seek to know God, and faith comes naturally.

If we want a vital experience with God, we must not sit passively by, hoping for some visitation. Action must be taken. We must discipline our lives. Taking time to seek God in prayer, reading His Word, and giving opportunity for Him to speak to our hearts, must become a daily habit.

To know God changes everything. It not only gives you a sense of unworthiness, but brings an awareness of the availability of His power.

Have you studied the lives of the great men of the Bible? Associated with the lives of these men I have noticed three common qualities. They were men of faith, peace, and power. This first attribute, faith, is the prerequisite of courage and living without fear. Notice this picture of the Psalmist: "Therefore will we not fear, though the earth do change, and though the mountains be shaken into the heart of the seas" (Psalm 46:2).

"The Lord is my light and my salvation; whom shall I fear? The Lord is the strength of my life; of whom shall I be afraid?" (Psalm 27:1-2).

God said to Daniel, "Fear not . . . be strong" (Daniel 10:19).

Listen to Paul: "If God is for us, who can be against us?" (Romans 8:31).

Secondly, these men enjoyed a deep, abiding peace. When faith comes and fear leaves, worry is gone and peace reigns. There is an absolute release from the tensions and the strain that often makes us powerless.

Thirdly, knowing God is also an experience of power. It is not something we achieve; it is something God brings with Him when He dwells in our hearts. What changed Moses from a leader of sheep to a leader of men? It was the result of knowing God and learning to commune with Him those forty years on the back side of the desert. Knowing Christ in His resurrection glory, the Apostle Simon Peter was able to shake free from his own weakness to go out and shake the world. Ask the Apostle Paul from whence came his power, and he answers, "From knowing Christ personally." To know God is to have faith, peace and power.

2. Study His Word

"So faith cometh by hearing, and hearing by the Word of God" (Romans 10:17).

"Blessed is the man that walketh not in the counsel of the ungodly . . . but his delight is in the law of the Lord; and in his law doth he meditate day and night" (Psalm 1:1-2).

Knowing and obeying God's Word develops strong faith. To know God's Word we must discipline ourselves to study and apply its teaching. Read Psalm 119 and notice how many times the Psalmist places emphasis upon self-discipline in order to read and understand God's Word.

> Thy word have I laid up in my heart, that I might not sin against thee . . . I will meditate on thy precepts, and have respect unto thy ways . . . I will delight myself in thy statutes: I will not forget thy word . . . Forever, O Jehovah, thy word is settled in heaven . . . Unless thy law had been my delight, I should then have perished in mine affliction . . . I will never forget thy precepts; for with them thou hast quickened me . . . I have refrained my feet from every evil way, that I might observe thy word . . . Through

thy precepts I get understanding . . . Thy word is a lamp unto my feet, and a light unto my path.

Live in His Word. Become familiar with what God has to say. Remember: the law of faith is that we first desire, and then determine if that desire is pleasing to God and not in conflict with His Word. How can we know unless we seek Him and know His will through the sacred Scriptures? Strong faith is developed by living in the Word.

3. Keep His Commandments

Disobedience makes cowards of us all. Obedience brings confidence and confidence is faith. Faith makes sense and brings results. God honors faith because faith honors God. John tells us, "Beloved, if our heart condemn us not, we have boldness toward God; and whatsoever we ask we receive of him, because we keep his commandments and do the things that are pleasing in his sight" (I John 3:21-22). In other words, we get whatever we ask because we are obeying Him and doing those things that please Him. To please Him we must "believe on the name of His Son, Jesus Christ:" and embodied in the word *believe* is obedience, for our Master said, "If a man love me, he will keep my word" (John 14:23).

God's Word should be our guide, our compass, and the scales on which we weigh ourselves. His instruction must be our way of life. If He says we are to do it, there is no other choice but to obey. If He says it is wrong to do a certain thing, there is no choice but obedience. Strong faith comes as a result of *doing* the things that are pleasing to God and *not doing* the things that are displeasing to Him.

4. Prove His Promises

Faith rests on facts. God is a fact; only "the fool hath said in his heart, there is no God" (Psalm 53:1). God's Word is fact and His promises are sure. "Heaven and earth shall pass away, but my words shall not pass away" (Matthew 24:35). A man whose faith is based on the fact of God and His never-failing promises holds his hand on the power-levers of the universe. Men fail, but God never fails. Faith in ourselves is important, but faith only in ourselves is not sufficient. A man about to crash in an airplane needs more than faith in himself. A condemned criminal being strapped into an electric chair needs more than faith in himself. Man must learn to direct his faith toward God, to touch the resources of the Infinite.

Faith in our fellow-man is of great value, but we must not stop there: I say this because it is difficult to forget his glaring failures of the past. Andrew Carnegie gave five million dollars to stop war. Failure followed. Have you trusted in some arm of flesh only to be cheated and defrauded? Often times the spoken or written word of our fellow-man is no good. The world is full of man's broken promises and unfulfilled pledges.

But faith in God is different. No man has ever found Him unfaithful or unwilling. If we will take time to know Him and obey Him and rely on His Word, all things are ours. This is how men got answers in Bible days, and this is the only way we will find answers today. God will not answer apart from our faith. Get the promises of God fixed in your heart. Get rid of every image or feeling that destroys your faith. Never permit a mental picture of failure to be in your mind. Remember, the foundations of your faith are the promises of God.

Exercise the faith you have. There is a divine law that what we do not use, we lose. Share with others what God has done for you. Write your relatives and friends, giving praise to God for answering your prayer. You will notice that as you begin to share with others, your faith will increase. Start applying faith in as many areas of your life as possible. Make it a hobby to gather faith by remembering the times that God has honored your faith.

Now, God will not transgress His law of faith nor work contrary to faith. *The more you use your faith the greater it becomes.* And the possibilities are unlimited. Your troubles may seem like giants, your rivers appear uncrossable. But whatever you do, don't forget His promises. Steal away in secret and pray, and begin to meditate on the many times He has helped you. God can be trusted. He can see better than you can, and He will work out things that are not now seen. So use your faith.

Remember also that faith is contagious. Associate with people who are "of like precious faith." Listen to their testimonies and experiences. Attend church where the preacher exalts God and His Word and reminds men that our God still lives today. Read biographies which relate the experiences of others, and be an attentive listener to the victories of those around you.

As you continue to use your faith, even though it is as small as a mustard seed, it will grow to become that which brings honor and glory in your Saviour. The secret of faith is faith *in God*.

DOES FAITH CHANGE THE RESPONSE OF GOD?

We all know that faith can do great things! Men who have had faith in themselves — faith in the ability of their hands and their minds — have brought into existence the seemingly impossible. Charles Jefferson said, "Faith is building on the invisible to accomplish the impossible." Man will eventually conquer space because he believes he can, just as Columbus and Dr. Jonas Salk believed in what they were attempting, and success became a reality.

The same is true in the spiritual realm. A father besought the Master, "If thou canst do anything, have compassion on us, and help us." His son was in desperate need of help. Jesus replied, "If thou canst believe, all things are possible to him that believeth" (Mark 9:22, 23). You see, the prime objective of such faith is to get things done, and faith can do the impossible. Have you noticed, where there was no faith nothing great was possible, and where there was faith, everything was possible. Why? Because faith is trust in the trustworthiness of God. It means confidence in God — in His Word.

Christian faith, then, is not merely a natural ability; it grows as a fruit of the Spirit, and when our faith makes contact with God we become partakers of the Divine nature. When our faith is in union with the Divine will, it makes all things possible to the believer. And faith in God carries with it a guarantee because it places confidence in the only One whose promises can be wholly depended upon.

The Bible leaves no doubt that faith does bring a response from God. No man should expect to get anything from God if he fails to believe. Doubt is a sin. In fact, nothing displeases God like questioning His ability to perform or His willingness to help. "Whatsoever is not of faith is sin" (Romans 14:23).

"Jesus said unto them, if ye have faith and doubt not, even if ye shall say unto this mountain, Be thou taken up and cast into the sea, it shall be done" (Matthew 21:21).

No prayer can be answered without faith, but faith utilized accomplishes even more than we can ask or think.

God has been good to His creation. No man can accuse God of being unjust, unfaithful, or a respecter of persons. He stands ready to help and longs to assist. One thing is clear in the Scriptures — He wants to do what He has promised. So, when the law of faith is carried out, results follow. If we want results from God and to share the benefits of His promises, we must obey the law of faith; God will keep His Word. Faith will never work contrary to the Word of God, the will of God, or the wisdom of God, but faith brings a response *from* God. If faith appears powerless, then it is not faith. You cannot have faith without results because faith always brings action and releases power.

The quality of our faith is determined by the object of our faith. This is why Jesus so often said to those around Him, "Have faith in God." When God is the object of our faith, the quality of our faith brings corresponding response from him.

Is This Faith Within the Reach of Every Man?

If the enemy can persuade us not to believe, he has won a great victory, because it is impossible for us to mature in our walk with God if we remain doubters, men and women of unbelief. Romans 12:3 says, "God hath dealt to *each* man a measure of faith." Faith is an attribute of man's created being, and when one becomes a new creature in Christ he begins to direct his faith to God and His Word. If we do not develop a strong and positive faith, it is our own fault. If faith in God made the men of Bible times truly great, is not that faith our big need today?

There is simply no mystery about the way to get faith. It is to expose oneself to God and His Word in obedience. Faith then becomes contagious. It inevitably spreads as we share it with others. Others will draw faith and inspiration from our lives as together we look to Jesus, "the author and perfector of our faith."

By faith we live. "That life which I now live in the flesh I live in faith" (Galatians 2:20).

By faith we walk. "For we walk by faith, not by sight" (II Corinthians 5:7).

By faith we stand. "Thou standest by faith" (Romans 11:20).

By faith we fight. "Taking up the shield of faith, wherewith ye shall be able to quench all the fiery darts of the evil one" (Ephesians 6:16).

By faith we dispel fear. "Why are ye fearful? O ye of little faith" (Matthew 8:26).

By faith we keep true to God. "Who by the power of God are guarded through faith unto a salvation ready to be revealed in the last time" (I Peter 1:5).

By faith we receive healing for our bodies. "Pray for one another that ye may be healed, and the prayer of faith shall save the sick" (James 5:15-16).

In fact, it is by faith that our faith grows and increases. "But having hope that, as your faith groweth, we shall be magnified in you according to our province unto further abundance" (II Corinthians 10:15).

Through every age faith has been the test which God has placed on every man. It has always been required of man to believe that God, our heavenly Father, wants the very best for each of us. That is still the basis of God's dealing with us. We prove God by our trusting, and we receive in accordance with our faith. If we believe God, His benefits are ours. He must be consulted and obeyed and not questioned. Take the faith He has given you and direct it back to Him and His promises, and watch it grow into a strong, mountain-moving faith.